Dear Yvonne,
   Thank you so much for your
Prodigious talents! I hope my own
work proves worthy of them!

SING TO ME
OF A WORLD TO WIN

Henry Howard

HENRY HOWARD

VAGABOND

VAGABOND

VENICE, CALIFORNIA

FAIR USE NOTICE

Published by VAGABOND
Mark Lipman, editor

VAGABOND Collection

Intellectual Property
Howard, Henry
Sing to Me of a World to Win
1st ed. / p.cm.

ISBN13: 978-1936293-30-8

Made in the USA.

TABLE OF CONTENTS

AUTHOR'S PREFACE

SING TO ME OF A WORLD TO WIN is my second collection of human rights poetry. It is meant as both a sequel to, and a stand-alone volume to, my first such book, SING TO ME OF MY RIGHTS, also published by VAGABOND (2014). Like the poems in the first volume, these are poems of struggle and oppression, but also resistance. The world has become ever more difficult and dangerous since my first efforts in this direction, and some of the subjects and poems in this book are challenging, disturbing and painful. But always there is an underlying tone of optimism, of resistance, of the potential of indeed creating for all of us a world to win.

I find activism in poetry, and poetry in activism itself; the two are symbiotic, because poetry captures activism's commitment to bettering the human condition, but simplifies it and makes it accessible in the language of the heart. At the same time, activism is the poetry of loving humanity in an unconditional, universal way, and being willing to take responsibility for each other's well-being – with all the risks, challenges and rewards that come from loving, whether on an individual, or global, level. I have always believed in the power of words to heal, to lift up, to inspire one person or millions to march forward together into the future. That's why I joined the Revolutionary Poets Brigade, and why this volume, like my first, is highlighted by resistance to oppression, rather than just capturing the pain of injustice. Many of the subjects in this book are painful – but resistance lessens pain, because at least it provides a fighting chance, and without resistance and the optimism it generates, what are we? As Rabbi Hillel so hauntingly asked, "If not now, when?"

The greatest injustice of all is to bear witness to suffering, and do nothing (something Dr. King repeatedly warned us all about). Pastor Martin Niemoller, imprisoned in Dachau during World War II, experienced this firsthand: "In Germany, they came first for the Communists, but I didn't speak up because I wasn't a Communist. Then they came for the Trade Unionists, but I wasn't a worker, so I didn't speak up. Then they came for the Jews, but I wasn't a Jew, so I didn't speak up. Then they came for the Catholics but I was a Protestant, so I didn't speak up. Then they came for me – and by that time, there was no one left to speak up. In order to prevent this from ever happening again, injustice against anyone, anywhere, must become the concern of everyone, everywhere!" Never give up, never back down. In the immortal words of Joe Hill, labor organizer and hero to the working class everywhere: DON'T MOURN, ORGANIZE!

INTRODUCTION

SING TO ME OF A WORLD TO WIN

> "With the poor of the earth I want to throw my destiny."
> ~ Guantanamera.

Henry Howard carries on the vision of Jose Marti, with this song of resistance in a time of sociopathic governance. He becomes incarnate with the person crying in the wilderness of oppression. His song is one of communion and the splendor of truth. Henry also writes with the legacy of Eduardo Galeano, telling the story simply and leaving the oppressors self condemned.

His call to, "join us." recalls the urgency of Otto Rene Castillo. While living in Guatemala on March 19, 1967 I was told of his death. He was burned at the stake following four days of torture and mutilation by the Guatemalan Army. His poetry, like that of Henry Howard's calls for a world to win through unifying poetry, love and action... resistance.

This history goes back to Tecún Umán who was also burned to death in the Mayan struggle against the conquistadores.

Then there is Victor Jara, another of Henry Howard's spiritual colleagues. You will meet Victor in *Sing to Me of a World to Win.*

And what is the song about in his new book of poetry *Sing to Me of a World to Win*? It is about internationalism. No more nation worship leading to the war racket. It is about resistance... hopefully nonviolent. It is about a mystique necessary for world unification: poetry, song and symbols of peace. It is about sports rather than biocide.

Our apology to those offended but there will be no silence about two trillion dollars set aside for nuclear suicide, nor the cholera camps of Yemen, nor the prison camp of Gaza, nor the scandal of our massive and unnecessary prisons, nor the tearing apart of families by systematic racism, nor the worst distribution of wealth on the planet to name just a few issues.

So thanks very much Henry for using your great gifts once again. We hear your call to sing. May we all be part of the lyrics!

~ Blase Bonpane

WE ARE ALL REFUGEES

"A nation ringed by walls will only imprison itself."

~ Pres. Barack Obama

SING TO ME
OF A WORLD TO WIN

I, the refugee,
wander the earth without respite
in search of a home,
ball and chain securely fixed
to my tired feet.

If you sing to comfort me as I wander,
sing loudly,
for I am nearly deaf to hope.
But if you persist in your own hope for me,
I can slowly start to learn the tune,
of how I have only my chains to lose
and a world to win.

It may seem like there is little to win.
If I am a black man in Libya,
my worth as a human being bid for $400
in the slave market of Tripoli,
sing until the ball and chain fall from my feet,
and I can run through the streets
unchecked and free!

If I am an American woman,
learning to say ME TOO
after a lifetime of silence about my sexual abuse,
sing to me how I have only the chains
of men's sexual power to lose,
and world of equality to win.

If I am Rohingya,
following the Burma Road from Myanmar
to Bangladesh,
my child strapped securely to my back
as my village burns behind me,
sing to me so my breast milk may not dry up
and make my daughter go hungry,
even as the world forgets me.

If I am from North Africa,
sailing to Sicily on a raft with 100 others,
adrift in the swells that menace us
with the salty taste of death,
sing to me of my rights that will break my chains,
and cast me towards a fertile shore
where I have my life to grow, and the world to win.

From the cholera camps of Yemen
and the Intifada camps of Gaza,
from the ghost city of Aleppo
to the great cities of Europe
whose streets are filled with ghosts
in search of a human home,
I, the refugee, must learn a new song
in a brave new world.

Sing to me of my rights
until my own throat calls them forth,
and with the rhythm of resistance
breaks the chains that bind me
and builds me a home in a world to win!

CITY OF GHOSTS

When night falls on Aleppo,
in what little is left of Syria,
the bombs stop just long enough
for the ghosts of the dead
and the living skeletons of the nearly-dead
to begin their slow-motion parade through the ruins.

Hand in hand, the invisible and the forgotten
move silently in the soft glow of candlelight,
for the power went out long ago
along with the light in their eyes.

The ghosts of Aleppo search the crumbled land
for the remnants of their lives,
while the still-breathing lifeless
stumble and pick their way through broken concrete,
and the fathomless holes of bomb craters
descending all the way to hell.

Starving in every inch of their bodies and souls,
the ghost-people raid an abandoned bakery,
but there is no bread in sight,
not even a solitary bag of white flour,
only an inch-thick layer of white dust.

On the top shelf a tempting crust beckons invitingly,
but it is guarded by an equally hungry spider,
who readies himself to pounce on the intruders.
Survival of the fittest.

The streets are as lonely and empty as a vast cemetery,
and the burned-out buildings stand like forlorn tombstones
over the countless dead.
With the rising sun,
the roar and whine of artillery eclipse the screams
of those still trapped.

The sky splits.
The air bellows.
The ground convulses.
The earth moans.

Meanwhile, who speaks for the children of Aleppo,
the defenseless slaughtered, or the modern Anne Franks,
in hiding from capture by soldiers whose side in the war
is as unknown as their names?

There is seven-year-old Bana, with mischievous eyes
and a gap-toothed smile,
who pleads with the world through her texted words
that this might be her last night on earth,
and why won't the world rescue her?

Or there is little Qumran,
who sits in the back of an ambulance,
his face bloody, his eyes staring like lifeless marbles.
Only he is alive, but too traumatized to even cry,
an image that leads a veteran newscaster to cry for him.

We, the viewing audience, watch transfixed,
as 30 seconds of horror
slowly fade from our televisions screens,
and our own tears, unshed, pool at the limits of our vision.

Aleppo is our generation's Guernica,
a slaughter of the innocent in a peaceful Basque town,
spurring the world's conscience to action,
but allowing us the escape of inaction
until there is no one left to kill.

Who will remember Guernica today,
as the men of Aleppo are shot or beheaded,
and the women and girls are raped
or sold as brides for the Islamic Caliphate of ISIS.

Ten years from now,
we will read commentaries in newspapers,
and safely relive the horror in documentaries,
and President Assad will spread his power far and wide
throughout the Middle East,
and become a great trading partner with us,
for that is the way of history, rewritten by the victors.

And the little spokespeople of the United Nations
will bow and scrape and press each other's hands for photo-ops,
then carry their briefcases full of notes to conferences,
and congratulate themselves for talking Aleppo to death
but saving the last 200,000 citizens
who disappeared in long lines of gray and blue buses
to an unknown fate.

Out of sight and out of mind, their human status
diminishes inexorably
from "Residents" to "Evacuees" to "Refugees,"
whose past is a dead city,
and whose future is an endless question mark,
because the journalists and camera crews have all gone home.

At last the long guns will fall silent and rusty over Aleppo,
and the bombers with their payloads of death
will fly high and remote like sleek carrion crows
in search of fresh road kill.
The grass will grow tall and untended over the ruins of Aleppo,
and the tombstones will crumble in the dustbin of history,
for when do the living ever remember a city of ghosts?

WHO WOULD
MUHAMMAD BOMB?

When President Bush declared from the rubble
of the World Trade Center,
"The people who knocked down our buildings
will hear from us very soon!"
I knew that the next day we would be at war with Islam,
and I thought, "Our grief is not a cry
to knock down other people's buildings.
Who would Muhammad bomb?"

When our missiles rained death from above
on Iraq's towns and open-air markets,
I knew that we were still at war with Islam,
and I asked myself again,
"But who would Muhammad bomb?"

President Bush piously declared,
"We are not at war with Islam,"
as he rounded up 5,000 innocent Muslims
and condemned them without charges or trial
to disappear in secret detention camps.

And I opened my copy of the Qur'an,
and read of Allah, the Beneficent, the Most Merciful,
the Most Compassionate, and I silently prayed
to the warmongers and revenge seekers,
"Who would Allah and his Messenger of Peace,
Muhammad, bomb?"

The people who choose open-ended war with Islam
have never read the Qur'an that I have studied.

The Christian extremists who loudly proclaim,
"Not all Muslims are terrorists, but all terrorists are Muslims!"
And stage cartoon contests that depict Muhammad
with the snout of a pig
have never read the Qur'an like I have.

Likewise, no Jewish extremists on the West Bank
who burn mosques and blow up Arab houses
have studied the Qur'an with the same compassion
for the soul that they reserve for Torah.
If they did, they might ask a simple question
that could stop the killing forever:
"If Abraham is the Father of Islam as well as Judaism,
would he and Muhammad bomb each other?
After all, they are brothers!"

And the same message is meant loud and clear
for the followers of radical Islam,
who proclaim devotion to Allah and Muhammad
but rape twelve-year-old girls as the spoils of war,
and force eight-year-old boys to behead hostages,
and celebrate their fealty to a God of blood:
Muhammad was a prophet of peace, social justice,
and women's rights. Who would Muhammad rape?
Who would Allah bomb?

Today, it seems I am a Muslim,
escorting my Jewish neighbor's children
to a school where they learn only co-existence
with my son and daughter, not hatred.

And today, I am an observant Jew,
discussing Islam with a Muslim baker two streets down,
reading in the cool sanctuary of his mosque
how the Qur'an echoes the words of the Talmud:
The one who saves a life, saves the world entire.

And today I am also a Christian
who every Sunday, after church, buys asthma medicine
for the ten-year-old daughter of a Somali window washer,
who lost his job when the scaffolding fell and crushed his legs.

I am all these things and more,
at a time when a single push of a button
can blow us all to the gates of Paradise.
But the right words, spoken softly and with love,
can unite us all: "Who would Allah bomb?
Who would Adonai bomb?
Who would Jesus bomb?
Who would Abraham bomb?
Who would Muhammad bomb in the name of peace?"

TICKET TO ANYWHERE, DESTINATION NOWHERE

Last night, my car radio played an old Paul Simon song
that seemed achingly new:
"I'm sitting in the railway station,
got a ticket for my destination."

As I sang the lyrics to "Homeward Bound,"
I thought of the refugees
sitting in the railway stations of Europe
bound for anywhere except home,
begging for a ticket to anywhere,
even a destination stamped "Nowhere."

By the tens of thousands they are coming,
month upon month,
marching forward with only hope to sustain them,
the shadow people with only the clothes on their backs,
even on the brightest day nameless, faceless, invisible
to a world with a million reasons not to see
a million souls that remind us too much of ourselves.

Germany says they cannot take anymore,
France says to keep them away from its own borders,
Hungary has built a sinister fence of razor wire,
and everyone looks to Turkey, already bursting at the seams
with the human debris of Arab Springs and African wars.

Meanwhile, the world gazes with wondering eyes at America,
where a young poet once welcomed
"The wretched refuse of your teeming shores,"
but whose own shores may soon bristle with an electric fence
2,000 miles long, to hold back the tide
of unaccompanied children and invisible laborers
whose dreams fade with every step.

The refugees now flooding Europe have been walking
for more than three years,
yet the world pretends it is surprised
at the staggering numbers
it now claims it cannot absorb.

A million flee the war in Syria,
while the U.N. debates and President Assad laughs,
because he knows the great leaders are more afraid
of radical Islam than of stable dictators
who slaughter only their own.

In Libya and Egypt,
the crooked kings are gone,
yet the keys to the kingdoms
have already been stolen by the well-armed elites
who used the masses as fodder to tear down the walls.

The refugee crisis is everyone's problem,
when the engine that drives it is a system of power
that lines the pockets of the wealthy
with the spoils of war.

It is everyone's problem when the unspoiled gems
of the Mediterranean suddenly find their beaches tainted
by human suffering that sends tourists fleeing
and dollars vanishing,
and the bodies of two-year-olds wash ashore
to shock the adult world to briefest action.

It is everyone's problem because each of us
could be the next refugee
in a world with no room for us,
leaving us with no place
but the platforms of endless railway stations,
begging for a tattered ticket to anywhere,
even a destination stamped "Nowhere."

LIVES ON THE BORDER,
LIVES IN THE SHADOWS

They are drawn to our border like a magnet
by the thousands each year,
a human train
inching forward on tracks 2,000 miles long,
from the tin-roofed hovels of Central America
to the river that divides our world from theirs
like an inland sea.

No underground railroad this time,
they are visible for every mile of their journey,
only to be resigned to lives in the shadows
if they make it this far,
fueling our hidden economy
of gardeners, waiters, janitors,
nameless laborers who toil in the burning sun,
pouring the cement for a new hotel
or restaurant or luxury apartments.

The ones who are caught before they hitch rides
to the construction projects of Dallas or Houston,
or the orange groves of Florida,
or the grapevines of California,
languish for a day or a year in an INS detention camp,
until an old school bus dumps most of them back in Mexico,
or a plane without movies or music or menus
flies the Central Americans home to the misery they left behind.

And now there are multitudes of children
who arrive by themselves,
still crying for their parents
after a journey through three countries
and an end of innocence.

Why do they risk it all,
those of such tender years?
Because Honduras has one of the world's
highest murder rates,
and in Tegucigalpa,
Mara Salvatrucha beat Antonio to a pulp
and tried to make him join a gang
that murdered his best friend before his eyes.

Because in Guatemala,
Maria hid under her bed
and watched soldiers rape her mother,
and now speaks only in a whisper
and cannot bear to be held, or even touched.

Because Pedro from El Salvador
rode the train everyone calls "The Beast"
all the way from Chiapas,
but his brother, Miguel, was not so lucky:
he fell asleep, and fell between the cars,
and now he is just a bloody spot
in the Mexican dust.

The children who somehow stagger across the Rio Grande,
deep and wide and treacherous,
are easy fodder for La Migra,
who wait on the hill above,
in a scene so familiar
it has become background fodder for the nightly news.

But is it familiar to deposit children
in pre-fabricated warehouses,
to hastily feed and clothe them,
then process and deport them like prisoners,
when they are accused of no crime?

While our government argues and stalls and haggles
over dollars and cents
until our immigration policy makes no sense at all,
the children sit idly, day after day,
just inside our border now,
in the United States at last,
but the invisible border between them and us
will be hard to cross, indeed.

The past still bubbles to the surface
like noxious ooze
in their memories or nightmares,
while the future is nothing but a question mark.

Most of all, their present remains an exclamation mark
of sadness and confusion,
signposts to a destination
where nothing is certain but the uncertain paths
of lives on the border, lives in the shadows.

THE NEW WARSAW GHETTO

As Israeli bombers turn night into day
and tank shells indiscriminately set ablaze
whole apartment blocks, schools, markets,
even hospitals and U.N. shelters,
my mind is ablaze with images of the burning
of another ghetto, seventy years before.

Let us call the Gaza Strip what it is:
The world's largest modern ghetto,
while Israel, born from the very ashes
of the Warsaw Ghetto,
has given birth to this lion's-den of suffering,
and brandishes the whip and the key
of the lion-tamer and ghetto gatekeeper alike.

In 1940's Warsaw, there was a high wall
capped with splinter glass and razor wire.
In Gaza, there is a high wall of stainless steel,
capped by razor wire, high-tension lamps,
and the very latest in surveillance gear.
Meanwhile, the Palestinian Authority,
Israel's faithful puppet in the West Bank,
serves as the new Judenrat, the Jewish Council of Elders,
who decide at Israel's behest
whose houses in Gaza will be bombed or raided,
and who gets the crumbs tossed out
by the Occupation government.

There are differences, of course,
between the Warsaw Ghetto and Gaza City Ghetto.
No deportation trains line the streets of Gaza City,
waiting to bear the Palestinians to a Middle East Treblinka,
and the bombings and firestorms are spaced a few years apart.

The United Nations has a nominal presence here,
though it is often ignored at Israel's whim.
The smell of freshly baked bread lines the streets,
and even in Gaza, children kick soccer balls
down alleys clogged with debris from the latest missile strike.

But the ominous parallels are there,
all too clear for those with open eyes to see a past
that is unforgiveable, and a present
that is unacceptable.

In the Warsaw Ghetto and its death-camp exits,
half a million souls starved in underground bunkers,
or breathed their last
in cold brick shower rooms filled with gas.

In the ghetto of Gaza City,
65% are malnourished,
100% go to bed hungry,
50% are unemployed,
90% depend on foreign aid,
while the borders, food, medicine,
and even the right to fish in the sea are controlled
by corrupt Egypt and Imperialist Israel.

The Warsaw Ghetto Uprising
and the Palestinian intifadas alike
were children's wars,
waged by 10, 11 and 13-year-olds armed with rocks
and gasoline bombs,
against tanks and automatic weapons forged in the iron
of Capitalist occupation and nation-stealing.

What is needed is a new kind of intifada,
waged on both sides of the Gaza City Ghetto
by Palestinians and Israelis,
with their chains to lose and a world to win!

The wall that slices through lemon trees and olive groves,
separates families and divides neighborhoods,
and enforces apartheid between two peoples
with no historical need to be enemies
except beneath the tyranny of state power,
cannot survive a battering by a people awakened
by their shared oppression.

On that day,
the ghosts of the Warsaw Ghetto
and the ruins of the Gaza City Ghetto
will share the pain, and the memory,
and even the triumph of history,
as the Red Crescent and the Star of David
fly high above one Palestine,
united at last!

I'M SO ANGRY, I CAN'T BREATHE!

When I saw the cellphone video of Michael Brown,
lying in his own blood for six hours
on a Missouri mean street
until a coroner's van hauled him away
like just another road kill,
I was so angry that I put my hands up.

But no one shot me.

When I saw the video of Eric Garner
being taken down forever in a chokehold
for all the world to see and gasp over
as his own breath left his body,
I got so angry I couldn't breathe!

Only, I got my breath back as soon as the video faded.

Between those two pressure points
of blue violence on black lives,
Ferguson, Missouri exploded in flames
and New York City and a handful of other cities
exploded in the flames of a new civil rights movement
with an old refrain: BLACK LIVES MATTER!

I remember marching to police headquarters in Los Angeles
in the 1980's and 90's,
bearing the photos of dozens of black lives
cut down by LAPD, NYPD, and other police
around the country
under color of authority.

Back then we called it the Stolen Lives Project,
because wherever it happens,
stolen lives matter.
Black lives matter.
Women's lives matter.
Human lives matter.

Who can forget the handcuffed frame
of Oscar Grant,
his life's-blood staining the platform
of a crowded San Francisco subway station,
with a hole in his chest the size of a welder's tank
from the cop who claimed he mistook his own gun
for a non-lethal taser?

Stolen lives matter.
Black lives matter.
Michael Brown's life mattered.
Eric Garner's life mattered.
Oscar Grant's life mattered.

In Cleveland, Ohio a cop
with a history of anger management problems
pulled to a sidewalk where 12-year-old Tamir Rice
played happily with a toy air pistol.
In two seconds, without asking a single question,
the cop fired one round and took that child out.
You see, his bullet was real.
And that black boy's death was real. And irreversible.

Black lives matter.
Women's lives matter.
Children's lives matter.
Stolen lives matter.

And then there was Eric Garner,
a 350-pound gentle giant, black as a man could be,
walking the hot pavement in a Brooklyn summer,
peddling loose cigarettes for some loose change.

Last time I checked, cigarettes don't fire bullets.
Maybe they're a crime against people's health
for stealing their breath,
but they just don't seem worth choking someone to death over.

But the cop who took him down
in a chokehold that made one gasp just to watch
disagreed, and ignored him for half an hour
as he lay face-down and pleaded over and over,
"I can't breathe!"
And then he really couldn't,
and by the time the coroner came,
all the wind that propelled his pleas and his sobs
and his last breath
was gone and limp like the sails of a ship
caught in the Doldrums.

And when Eric Garner was no more,
I got so angry I threw my hands in the air
and I, too, just couldn't breathe!

Eric Garner's mother said on television.
"It's not a black/white thing,
it's a police thing!"

She got it right.
It's a blue on black thing,
and sometimes even a blue-on-white thing.
It's a no-accountability thing under cover of authority.

When black lives don't matter,
cities burn.
They burned in Los Angeles in 1965
and again in '92,
in Ferguson in 2014,
and, for the moment, just beneath the surface
in New York, and a hundred other cities from coast to coast.

As long as black lives don't matter,
and women's lives don't matter,
and children's lives don't matter,
and stolen lives don't matter,

They're not regarded as fully *human* lives.
They can be cut down like summer wheat
without the gunmen, under color of lawmen,
being finally held to account.

It will indeed be a police thing
under cover of impunity,
and I will be so angry I'll keep putting my hands up
until one day, I too, can't breathe.

But I will go out with my fist in the air
and my voice loud on the wind,
and I will not be just another life stolen
under color of the thin blue line,
because I, too, am a human being –
and human lives matter!

Everyone's Blood is Red

On a quiet June night,
the Devil went to church in Charleston.
He did not come with cloven hooves and a tail,
but with the quiet deception of a lost young man
pretending to seek understanding
in the ways of God.

In his heart he was an angry white man,
but he told the twelve peaceful black men and women
that he wanted to know their God,
and asked to share their bible study with them.

They rose with one body,
and welcomed him to their house of the Lord.
But when their study of the Good Book was over,
the stranger who sojourned with them
opened a new chapter of evil.

There was no doubt about the facts,
no shades of gray except the unfathomable why
to layer the investigation.
Nine lay slaughtered amidst the pews,
and the youthful killer confessed with ease
to the three worshippers he had spared.

The case was as simple as black and white:
He had come to this historic black church
to start a race war,
but he failed to grasp that everyone's blood is red.

Beneath his white skin filled with disbelief
in the brotherhood of Man
and the bullet-riddled black skin of true believers
in a God of love and mercy, not revenge,
the blood of a racist and the blood of his victims
was the same.

How can one start a race war
when everyone's blood is red
and there are no separate races,
only the rainbow of colors
that make the human race shine like the sun?

The Devil went to church in Charleston,
but ordinary people came in their thousands
to give the Devil his due:
All ages, all faces,
all cultures, all races,
black and white, red, yellow and brown
have sworn to rebuild this house of love
from the ashes of hate to hallowed ground.

How can there be a race war
when all our genes come from Lucy,
mother of us all,
a black woman of Africa who stirred a cooking fire
at Olduvai Gorge a million years before?

The answers aren't always as simple
as black and white,
but when everyone's blood is red,
people can respond to hate
with love instead of might.

How else can we explain
the redeeming force of the victims' families,
who rebuffed the killer's screaming words,
"I hate you!"
With a soft, quiet answer for all the world to hear:
"We forgive you!"

Maybe the unity in Charleston
was just a kumbaya moment for the cameras,
to cover up feelings better left unsaid.

But I choose to believe that those who wept
and held hands with colors different from their own
prayed the Devil back to Hell,
when they declared that love is universal
and everyone's blood is red.

WOMEN ON FIRE

It was a cold, unpleasant day
in New York, that gray March 25, 1911,
but the old Asch building at MacArthur and Greene
squared its concrete shoulders, and shrugged off the chill.

High above, on the eighth through tenth floors,
the women inside were unaware of the weather;
it belonged to the outside world, off-limits to them
until the first shadows of night.

Their world consisted of the windowless walls
of the Triangle Shirtwaist factory,
whose young employees cut and sewed blouses
by the thousands for seven to twelve dollars a week.

Somewhere on the eighth floor,
a fire took form then unstoppable life,
in a scrap bin holding the detritus of sweatshop labor.
Hundreds of pieces of bright cloth and fabric
lay uncollected and forgotten,
just like the women who turned them
into something beautiful.

When the burning began, a frantic call from the eighth floor
gave warning to those on the tenth,
but the ninth floor was already ablaze
like the Ninth Circle of Hell.
The fire consumed as it climbed,
spreading orange fingers toward a fearsome embrace
with the frantic survivors on the roof.

There were elevators, but they were full within minutes.
There were exit doors,
but the owners kept them locked during working hours
to prevent unauthorized breaks, or thefts of the sacred cloth,

or the forbidden fruit of cigarettes,
smoked through the fabric.
There was a fire escape, old and unreliable
as the factory owners themselves,
and it soon collapsed under the weight of bodies
who clung to it like grapes, until falling in twisted bunches
to the scorched pavement below.

Soon there was but one way out
for the dozens of women and men
with no earthly exit.

One by one or two by two,
holding hands to give them courage,
women and girls appeared at the crackling windows,
young Jewish and Italian immigrants willing to climb
the ladder of success rung by rung
through the horror of sweatshop labor.

Of the 123 women and 23 men
consumed by the Triangle fire,
sixty two ushered in the era of jumpers:
A man was seen kissing a woman in silhouette,
before they were married to the flames.

There was little Kate Leone
and her best friend Sarah Rosario Maltese,
14-year-year olds whose short lives
and long journey to America
ended in a fierce embrace beneath a blanket of fire.

By the end of the long day,
the last embers twinkled in the breeze
like the glow of freshly-lit cigarettes,
and mingled with the soft gray ash and even whiter snow
to lend a cloak of dignity to the charred forms
on the cobblestones far below.

They were the first, these sixty two jumpers,
but they have not been the last.
When the World Trade Center crumbled
in the terror attacks of 9/11,
there were those who cheated death from above
by taking a long leap into eternity.

There was the office worker, who placed a forlorn call
to his wife of three decades,
only to find her answering machine on;

There was the master chef in the restaurant
called Windows on the World,
who cooked a fabulous omelet for the last time
before jumping from the frying pan to escape the fire;

And there was the young woman,
whose death jump was caught forever
in a freeze-frame image
of an awful moment in time:
In a last-ditch effort to preserve her dignity,
she straightened her skirt and tugged it modestly
over panties no one could see but her.

No one can begin to grasp what it was like
to open the smoke-stained windows
and gaze at the world far below,
before slipping the bonds of earth
and riding the wind on wings of eagles.
The endless days of burning steel
and nights of broken glass
were my generation's Triangle Fire.

When I was a student at NYU,
I took a statistics class in that long-ago death factory
and never knew where I was,
for the desks and sewing machines had been replaced
by chalkboards and overhead projectors,
and not even a memorial plaque
adorned this edifice of tragedy.

Some good actually came from that century-old inferno.
Dozens of progressive laws sprouted like mushrooms
across the conscience of the labor landscape:
A shorter workweek, better pay, greater safety,
and a strong new union to fight for it all.

It was a blaze that sparked an unquenchable movement
of worker's rights and women's rights.
But why does it still take,
from the remote factories of Bangladesh
to the modern sweatshops that rise unseen
in the high-rises of Los Angeles,
women on fire to spread flames of justice
that can never be extinguished?

LIGHT TWO CANDLES

As Hannukah sends forth its light
to roll back the darkness in our lives,
light two candles to drive away the shadows
in men's and women's lives.

Light one candle for the courage of women,
who have lit their own way forward to the future.
Light one candle for the men in their lives
who have shared the long and winding road,
not leading the way, but walking as partners side by side.

Light one candle for every woman,
in the silence of sexual harassment or abuse,
who is silent no more,
and whose steadfast voice
shakes her chains of bondage loose.

Light one candle for every man
who refuses to hide in an ivory tower,
and use gender or position
to make women cower.

Light one candle for every woman
who speaks truth to power,
to call forth the power of Sisterhood.
And light one candle for every man
who gives up his false power
to free both sexes – if he only would.

Light two candles side by side
for the bravest of both sexes who walk together,
talk together, understand together,
and with one voice, as women and men,
shout down the darkness with two little words:
NEVER AGAIN!

LEADER OF THE FREE WORLD, LEADER OF NONE

*"Never be afraid to raise your voice for honesty
and truth and compassion against injustice and lying
and greed. If people all over the world... would do this,
it would change the earth."*

~ William Faulkner

TAKE A KNEE, MR. PRESIDENT, AND BOW TO THE WILL OF THE PEOPLE

When football players went down on one knee
before their games,
and The Star-Spangled Banner
that blared on loudspeakers
could not drown the silence of their protests,
you intercepted their gesture of defiance, and interrupted
the very heart of a campaign rally for a loyal friend.

"Any player who disrespects our flag
should be thrown off the field,
and fired! You're fired!" You trumpeted,
with the fury of the most famous line
from your reality TV show.
Only there was an air of complete unreality
to your whole response.

When hurricanes ravaged our country,
You stormed instead about a type of protest
you gave more publicity to
than the gesture itself.

As a budget battle took shape
with the fate of millions in the balance,
you budget more time to call for the punishment
of athletes who bore you today
for not hitting hard enough.

Free speech and speaking out
are as American as our flag and anthem.
Do you not grasp that this protest form of free speech
speaks out more eloquently
than a patriotic poem set to a nearly unsingable tune?

In the land of the not-so-free-for-everyone,
our flag has too often been a symbol of racial injustice
instead of color-blind liberation.
To take a knee is not to disrespect
a square of brightly woven cloth,
it is to say what needs to be said
in the home of the brave.

But how can you understand this special pain,
Mr. President,
when modern Nazis marched in Charlottesville,
bearing the swastika and the Confederate cross
beside the Stars and Stripes,
and you loudly proclaimed that "very fine people"
were among them, too?

When I learned the Pledge of Allegiance
and the Star-Spangled Banner,
I was not raised by my parents to pledge my loyalty
to a piece of fabric,
but to the words on paper called the Constitution,
the moral fabric that holds our country together.

Yes, I put my childhood hand on my heart
for the Star-Spangled banner,
but it was a broken heart for all the slaves
who fought that battle,
yet who were still shadow-people
in the land of the free.

Listen to the American people, Mr. President,
and you may learn that bent knees
can speak more loudly than words,
and sing more loudly than any anthem.

Football players are tired
of being treated like footballs,
when racism daily rides the wind of their lives
like a "hail Mary" pass,
and the very police who guard the game
may afterwards shoot a black player
they mistake for a burglar.

Take a knee, Mr. President,
and ask the turf to unlock its secrets.
Take a knee, Mr. President,
and see only a nation standing proud and tall,
and with one voice demanding liberty,
and justice for all.
Take a knee, Mr. President,
and bow to the will of the American people.

THE PRESIDENT AND THE BLUEBIRD

The tweet-tweet-tweet of your favorite bluebird
begins as music to your ears at 4 a.m.,
as your fingers fly in the solitude of the Oval Office
across computer keys,
composing the special tongue
with which you speak to the nation.

Only you know why the caged bird sings
your innermost thoughts before the dawn's early light.
The lonely tunes of Twitter's bluebird
beg to be played for the American people,
and for citizens throughout the globe, tuned in for words
to light the darkness of their political lives.

It is hard to express thoughts that inspire actions,
and actions that affect the entire world,
in 140 typed characters or less,
but that is your favorite way of address.

In a world where dialogue is reduced to Gigabytes,
our opinions are reduced to sound bites,
and global disputes can be dismissed as Malware Bytes.

Try to talk to us, Mr. President,
in the language of the heart
and the power of spoken words,
and let us judge both for ourselves.

Put the bluebird to rest, Mr. President,
and let justice tweet in words so sweet,
from your very lips,
to hide no more behind
the tweet-tweet-tweet of computer chips!

MOVING STONES, REWRITING HISTORY

For seventy years,
the stars and stripes have flown side by side
with the Star of David,
in Tel Aviv, the Hill of Spring.

Now, to fulfill a campaign pledge
that no one took seriously,
our President decides it is time
to rewrite history, and move our embassy
to Jerusalem, the City of Peace that is anything but.

Jerusalem was born
in ancient Palestine,
hewn from stone and plowed from sod,
but seen by millions as the throne of God.

No nation on earth recognizes Jerusalem
as the one true capitol of Israel.
Every nation that recognizes Israel,
and there are no longer so many of those,
sees Jerusalem as Palestinian land,
shared by Arabs and Jews alike,
united only by a single demand.

But you, Mr. Trump,
have decided on your own
that Jerusalem belongs
to Israel alone.

When the city was reunited
in 1967,
it was reunified by war,
and not by choice.

The world has long held
that the final status of Jerusalem's fate
should be settled through peace,
and not by hate.

Arabs, Christians and Jews
all share the same deep longing,
to speak of Jerusalem
with a sense of belonging.

No embassy resides
in the City of David,
and up to now no move was planned.
But you, Mr. Trump, have rewritten the history
of this divided land.

You have just ended peace
with the stroke of a pen.
No Palestinian will trust us again.
Instead of a committed partner for peace,
you have just chosen sides in a war without end.

Keep our embassy in Tel Aviv,
where all other nations have one.
Let Jerusalem stay like Vatican City:
Eternal Capitol to All, Capitol to none!

PEOPLE WHO FIGHT AND INSPIRE ME

"Hate cannot drive out hate. Only love can do that. Darkness cannot drive out darkness. Only the light can do that."

~ Dr. Martin Luther King Jr.

EARLY EVENING, AT THE LORRAINE MOTEL

At one minute past six,
Dr. King opened the door of room 306,
and stepped to the balcony of the Lorraine Motel,
for a breath of fresh air before he fell.

The April breeze was cool that night,
the evening ripe for a fresh new start.
As King stepped outside, his mind was clear,
with peace in his heart.

Only one night before,
he had told his listeners of a vision to trust:
He had seen the Promised Land
and would lead them there,
though the journey was long
and struggle they must.

As he closed the door of room 306,
the street was quiet, the nearby buildings quieter still.
How could he know, or did he,
that a man lay in wait to stop his heart,
and silence him colder than winter snow?

The rifle crack brought friends outside,
to point at a rooftop and look to the sky.
King's face was torn, his pulse was weak,
but his spirit was strong and could not die.

Who hasn't seen that famous photo
of King cradled in the arms of those he loved,
comrades pressing the wound of his shattered face,
while others pointed at a nearby building
where hate had filled the empty space.

A half-century has passed
since that moment in time
frozen forever at the Lorraine Motel.

Fifty years, and what have we learned?
Have we all moved forward,
or only been burned?

The answer still lies in the middle,
so near,
but the Peaceable Kingdom
is not yet here.

Riots have set
our cities aflame,
and in too many hearts
the hate is the same.

But history moves forward
regardless of pain,
when a whole people stand
and shout out their name

"Hate cannot drive out hate.
Only love can do that!"
Dr. King told the world
of the power of that.

The Lorraine Motel is a museum today,
across from the building that hid James Earl Ray.
One man has been silenced, but never his call.
Dr. King will still lead us to justice for all!

THE MUSIC DIDN'T DIE

It was cold on that early December night,
and I wondered if snow would dim the sunrise.
I tucked the blanket beneath my chin,
and watched the news with weary eyes.

Suddenly the anchor, with evident shock,
told all her listeners, awake or not,
that a legend had been murdered:
John Lennon had been shot.

As the details rumbled across the dials,
people gathered across the miles.
I had to join them,
and as snowflakes drifted from mournful skies,
I dressed in haste,
my own tears stinging my frightened eyes.

A cabbie and I sang "Imagine" a dozen times
as we rode through the paths of Central Park,
grief staining our frozen cheeks,
in the winter wind and consuming dark.

We found the gathering crowd,
heard quiet sobs as candles burned.
The driver turned to me and said,
"There is no charge, my friend. I play guitar,
and from Lennon's music I first learned."

As I joined the line a thousand strong,
even the trees looked lost and forlorn.
How could I, a stranger, make the crowd believe
that I, too, was hurt and wanted to mourn?

200,000 shell-shocked fans
filled Central Park's Great Bandshell.
A city magnet for concerts and joy,
enough music history to fill a museum,
now it rose like a high-domed tomb and mausoleum.

Numbing wind and scudding clouds
chilled our bones and blocked the sun.
But Lennon's music warmed our souls,
and healed our broken hearts as one.

The music didn't die
on that night of hate.
A bullet ended one man's songs,
but not his universal fate.

We raised every voice
to give peace a chance,
even as a man of peace
was silenced by a gun.

They say we all were dreamers,
but our crowd was not the only one.
We knew the music would unite us,
and the world will live as one!

One Man's Alliance
is Our Survival

You stood one evening on the gently rocking pier
in Venice, California,
and watched the sunset
as late-day fishermen gathered in their lines.

Suddenly you felt a chill
as pointed as the February wind,
as the sun dipped below clouds that loomed
like the broad anvils of a nuclear mushroom.

In that moment, you knew your life had changed.
They say one man can make a difference,
but you are one man who forged alliances
that can save our planet.

From the gates of Diablo Canyon
to the haunted earth of the Nevada Test Site,
to the gates of power
in our nation's war-obsessed capitol,
you marched, sat in, protested and campaigned
endless hours,
to save us from ourselves.

On my birthday, March 1st, 1986,
what better present could you give me
when you walked from sea to shining sea
to ensure that I could march
for dozens of birthdays more.

Throughout the years of nuclear menace,
your love for the people went global and nuclear.
When personal love finally beckoned you
with a partner to save the world two-by-two,
your wedding canopy was no atomic cloud,
but a tree of life.

To this day, you hug trees
as readily as people,
knowing that all creatures of the earth
are endowed with feelings
and nurtured with the wisdom of our tears.

Every year you fast like Cesar Chavez,
knowing that with love, mindfulness
and strength of purpose,
we can feed our souls
and call out to a world hungry for change:
YES, WE CAN!

And when political repression rains down upon us
with mighty storms of fear and doubt,
you build a house where activists can organize
without a moment's fear of burning out.

We gather to celebrate your birthday,
Jerry Rubin,
but pay no heed to increasing years.
for you are eternal,
and your alliance with the earth
brings forth our love, and loudest cheers!

A Patient
Wind
of
Peace

For every mighty blaze of freedom,
there is a patient wind of peace
to keep the spark alive,
a gentle but persistent gale of hope to sweep
the world clear of its debris of war and fear.

While everyone knows the name
of Mother Theresa,
you are the quiet Sister Theresa,
who teaches the oppressed to liberate themselves,
who teaches the liberated to free humanity,
who feeds the hungry,
and feeds those hungry for the secrets
of building a better a world.

Your husband's name is pronounced
like the mighty blaze of justice
that helps to light the common fire,
and fights for those whom injustice keeps apart.
But you are the wind at his back
that keeps the flames alive and bright,
in the streets of protest and the sacred depths of the heart.

From the vast colonias of Chile's poor
to a soup kitchen in Santa Monica
that fills the belly
and serves love to the soul,
you are the wind that lifts the sails
of the Good Ship Bonpane,
on a voyage to make the world healed and whole.

Blasé is a brilliant thinker,
and a speaker who moves thousands
when the battle-lines are bristling.
But it is from you that the soldiers of peace
crave soft hugs and words of hope
when the battle quiets for the night,
banners fold, and bullets stop whistling.

Side by side,
a mighty blaze of freedom
and a patient wind of peace,
Blasé and Theresa,
a light that shines in the darkness,
a force for good that will never cease!

THE RAINS CAME,
BUT SO DID THE PEOPLE

Wind and rain rode into Texas
like the horsemen of the Apocalypse.
The terrified people looked up,
and in the black storm clouds
beheld a pale horse,
and the name that sat on him was Harvey,
and Hell and high water followed with him.

The skies opened up and the rain poured down,
a flood not seen since ancient times.
Cars were submerged and houses swallowed
to their rooftops.
Cities great and small – Houston, Rockport, Corpus Christi –
became signposts on a new map of nature's terror.

Scaly monsters swam in the mire,
and shelters strained
under Harvey's ire.

Yes, the rains came,
but so did the people.
Even as the gray skies cried for Houston,
thousands brought forth the dawn
of humanity at its brightest.

In the midst of a new Great Flood
that would have made even Noah tremble,
the boats that cruised the flooded streets
in search of people to rescue
became a thousand Noah's Arks.

Strangers reached out to strangers,
and everyone belonged to one true family.
Noah built his ark for two of every species,
and the modern vessels of mercy
fulfilled a long-ago command.

Countless pets, who could not shout their need
in any human tongue,
could only meow and chirp and bark
in the universal tongue of animal suffering,
but the humans heard and saved them, too.

At last the sun returned
and helicopters from everywhere
became flying fortresses of hope,
bearing survivors to places of care.

Yes, the rains came, but so did the people.
Those who rescued and those who were saved,
from every background, every race,
wore a single human face.

Hurricanes will form again
and hurl their fury
at Texas or Florida,
or somewhere in between.

But hope will bring the sun anew,
and no dove need seek out distant lands
to bring an olive branch
to weary hands.

The people will rise to the challenge
and hear the call,
of a global village
that unites us all!

WHEN EVEN THE WATERS CRY

Mni Wiconi, Water is Life!
The refrain of the Native people at Standing Rock
sweeps the prairie like the haunting North Dakota wind.
"Water is Life! Water is Life!" It is a cry we hear in our sleep,
and a clarion call for everything that walks
or crawls upon the earth,
even the bear and the mountain lion
who hunt the deer in the Black Hills,
to come to Standing Rock and defend
the sacred tears of the Great Spirit.

Yes, our one True Mother cries for us all:
For the land and its waters that hide the graves of the Elders,
whose ghosts have knowledge of things to come
that make them shift in their sleep
with the uneasy dreams of a future
threatened by the present;

When the breeze breaks the Sun-shine
on the meeting place of the Great Missouri
and the gentle Cannonball rivers,
our Mother cries with joy for all;

She cries for the young people
who have grown up on the reservation,
and reclaimed their birthright,
who plant maize by day, and by night
dance the eagle to sleep;

She cries for the souls of the young whites
who come to Standing Rock
with open hearts, and who learn the dance
of friendship and welcome.
That teaches them to walk in the Indian way of nonviolence,
and protection of the land that gives back so much;

And she cries for all those who would do so much good,
and love so deeply,

if they were not so afraid
of their own government's power to crush them
with tear gas, and rubber bullets,
and the cynical lie that physical force
can never be overcome by soul-force.

She cries special tears
for the disrespect of women by the militias
sent to arrest them,
who laugh, then chain them naked in dog cages for hours,
even in freezing weather.
Standing Rock has become an American Abu Ghraib.

Everyone comes to Standing Rock,
the young and the old, every face and every race,
Indians and whites, blacks and Mexicans.
Even our military veterans,
descendants of the very soldiers who threw the Native people
out of the country they inhabited first,
and forced them into guarded homelands like this one,
under treaties already broken before the ink had dried.

Everyone comes to Standing Rock,
the first great gathering of the tribes
since the entire Native American Nation girded itself
before the battle of Little Big Horn.
They were Navajo and Shoshone and Ojibwa, Crow and Blackfeet,
Oglala Sioux and Dakota Sioux and the Lakota Sioux,
under the leadership
of mighty Chief Sitting Bull himself.

They come from every tribe in the country,
and all the proud descendants of the Sioux as far back
as the days when the buffalo roamed in countless herds.

There is a war already under way here,
a battle for the future of our country,
and for the soul of the Great Spirit who cries for us all.
Yes, it is a war, whose spoils for the corporations that wage it

are the countless gallons of oil that flow
beneath the innocent river.

But at Standing Rock, it is a war fought with love
against the forces of greed who fire their weapons
without restraint.
There are no protesters here,
only water defenders.

After the sheriff's men soaked everyone
with fire hoses in 25-degree water,
after an eleven-year-old Indian girl was killed
with a rubber bullet,
and a gentle student from Queens had her arm blown off
with a well-aimed grenade,
the American veterans of Afghanistan and Iraq came
in a convoy of peace warriors 2,000 strong,
to lock arms and stand like a rock
between unarmed water defenders
and the bully defenders of black gold and hard green cash.

The militias backed down and the Army Corps of Engineers
refused to grant a permit to the corporate giants
to finish the pipeline!
We won that round, but the war is far from over.
The next President has stock in both companies,
so he may overturn the ban,
and we may all need to gather again.

It does not matter.

There are thousands who have not left since last spring,
and thousands more who have walked the trail of tears since.
The sturdy teepees and the bright blue tents jut defiantly
above the white Dakota blizzards,
for everyone comes to Standing Rock
and no one will leave,
for Water is Life!

We are the protectors of life, Great Spirit.
Water us with the wisdom of your tears.

A Name on the Wall

The Wall cuts through time and space alike,
its simple form rising to an apex that pierces
the seamless blending of the seasons
and the disharmony of weather,
in a symmetry the eyes cannot evade.

58,000 names adorn those twin triangles
of black granite:
An engraved roll call that will last forever,
as a tribute to that many American lives lost forever
in a war called Vietnam.

The visitors come to The Wall
with cameras and sketchpads,
roses and etching paper,
some leaning on crutches to replace a vanished limb,
others just leaning on each other for the strength to remember.

Up close and personal on a grey June morning,
I too beheld the seemingly impersonal rows of names and dates,
columns that force the viewer
to draw near,
to confront,
to contemplate,
to reconcile the few memories of a life cut short
with the immutable fact of a death that is forever.

I carefully searched the rows and the names
until my eyes, too, widened with the shock of recognition:
Panel 43w: 1st Lieutenant Joseph Bravin,
a young man with whom, as a child, I wished to play.

He was all of nineteen, still a lanky teenager,
yet he made the rank of Commissioned Officer
straight from Basic Training.
That pleased his father,

a four-star general during World War II
who never left the sun-kissed shores
of his North Carolina base.

June 20th, 1968: Joey began his tour "in country,"
another world entirely,
where the jungle closed over heart and home,
and only the screams of men dying for a cause
they forgot with their first firefight
penetrated the ceaseless clatter of enemy guns.

September 18th, 1968: 1st Lieutenant Joseph Bravin
came home in a box,
decorated with a simple American flag.
I remember that morning like it was yesterday,
because I was hanging out with his sister and my cousin,
in her New York apartment one floor below
where young Joey would never return.

I was only eight years old,
but old enough to understand the scream from his mother
that shook my cousin's walls,
old enough to run upstairs with my cousin
and Joseph's young sister,
old enough to remember her tears
and the way she hyperventilated,
old enough to watch his mother clutch
the soft flag to her breast
and wail from the depths of her broken heart.

His grave is all covered with flowers,
picked in fierce bright colors that reflected
a fine summer's day.
I can almost see Joseph's hands rising in supplication,
hear his cries as the newly-turned earth covered him,
"Momma, don't leave me! It's dark here,
and I can't find the way home!"

Many years have passed
since Joseph Simon Bravin bought his
in a place called Qangtri, South Vietnam.
I am older now, and could stand
on every street corner in America
and scream out my feelings about the senseless war
that left the living and dead alike still trying
to find their way home.

In the bible, God promises to build for His people
a Place and a Name,
so that none may forget the life that was,
and shall never pass this way again.

In Washington, D.C. there is such a place
where millions may come, and none may forget.
Here, where I shed real tears
for our multitudes of stolen youth,
the demanding earth shall not let me forget at all,
and 1st Lieutenant Joseph Bravin's name
is forever engraved
and honored,
and remembered,
on a black granite wall.

A Fine Day for the Beach

Abraham Grodsky peered through the dark mist,
as his landing craft approached the death zone
on the looming shore.

He clutched his rifle protectively to his chest
as the ping of bullets sliced the boiling sea,
and mingled with the screams of beardless soldiers
no older than himself.

It was the 6th of June, 1941,
a fine day for the beach.

They came from the farms of Iowa, the Kansas wheat fields,
the golden sands of California,
and the skyscrapers of New York.
For young Abraham, it was a long way indeed from
Bialystok to the Bronx,
a life-long journey for the Grodskys of Poland
to the Grodds of New York.

Before Omaha Beach, there was simply Omaha,
and Abe's best friend, Bob Sorensen,
was from that gentle Nebraska farm town,
where the greatest danger was from the mean old bull
that stared him down each day from behind a fence
that wouldn't hold back a kitten, let alone a cow.

Abe and Bob held hands and held their breaths,
as the cold Atlantic swirled around them.
Already the swells were stained the color of cranberry
with the blood of hundreds,
but the two boys pushed slowly on.

Gaining a foothold in the sand at last,
Abe hurled himself at the narrow shelter
of a fold of rock.
Around him, men fell like trees chopped down for lumber
without defense.

A mortar shell blew the right arm off Bob Sorensen,
trying to keep his balance on the blood-soaked ground.
He stared for a moment at the beautifully-formed limb
and the nub of bone that defined its loss,
then picked up the arm and ran towards Abe,
who waited for him with both his own arms outstretched.

The air was pierced by endless noise,
a symphony of horror.
But Abe was grateful for each explosion
that lifted the sand high around him
and stole his hearing one blast at a time,
for he knew that death would be marked by endless silence.

With the coming of evening,
the red sun broke in weak defiance
through the steaming curtain of fog and smoke,
casting indifferent light on the soft French countryside
and the harsh symmetry of thousands of unburied dead
on the cold sand.

As the first stars of twilight glittered
with their comfortless white fire,
Abe Grodd took off his helmet
and said a mourner's prayer for Bob Sorensen,
then tenderly buried his severed arm beside him.
He had shielded it protectively throughout the day's battle.

This gentle soldier from the Bronx,
whose parents were the Grodskys of Bialystok,
could not yet know that he was destined to survive,
destined to become the loving husband of my aunt Celia,
devoted father to my favorite cousin, Martha,
wise and kind uncle to me.

All he knew was that night at last
was drawing a blanket over scenes
he could not bear to remember,
bringing a mercifully short end
to a fine day for the beach.

THE SINGER
AND THE HAT-CHECK GIRL

The tall singer and the small hat-check girl
huddled in the shadows
of curved street lamps that looked like bones,
and made their plans in hurried tones.

In the 1940's, no white cab driver
would take a black man through Harlem's blight,
not even if his tuxedo bulged with money
from sold-out shows, night after night.

So my sweet aunt Ceil
played the role of reluctant spider,
week upon week,
luring the yellow cabs with her sidewalk calls
of a damsel far too pretty to ignore,
then motioning with the quickest nod of the head
at the partly-opened nightclub door.

Before she left the club to play her weekly role,
my aunt briefly squeezed Paul Robeson's hand,
then lifted her hat
from the ornate stand.

Such was the way of the world,
even in enlightened New York:
A Jewish girl from the Bronx, who cringed each day
from those who saw her religion as a sin
and a Black singer, admired everywhere for his baritone voice,
but welcome nowhere with his smokey skin.

The nightclub owner knew the score,
and slipped a $20 bill in Robeson's hand, then whispered,
"This should cover you now for Thursday's ride home,"
Robeson, so statuesque and dignified, swallowed his pride
and glanced backwards at the band.

A few patrons watched the encounter
with the silence of sympathy or disdain,
while the old piano player thumped his Harlem blues
to ease the moment of Robeson's pain.

My aunt squared her shoulders,
donned her hat,
and with hands on hips, stood by the curbside,
one of many chic women seeking a ride.

The ruse did not work well that night.
Three cabbies drove off with squealing tires,
leaving the singer to eat their dust,
while a fourth looked Robeson over with weary disgust.

"You can whistle for a ride, buddy," the cabbie said,
his voice a mix of fear and strife.
"Why not?" Robeson replied.
"I've sung for my meals each night of my life!"

The driver pulled away from the curb,
then stopped and returned for another view.
The night was hot and the rides were few;
Robeson at least could sing for his bread,
but the cabbie might have to whistle all night for a fare,
for all he knew.

"Come on, I'll take you,
and your songs can be my tip,"
said the cabbie, opening the door.

"See you Thursday night, Ms. Koffman,"
Paul Robeson bowed,
smiling broadly at my aunt once more.

"I can't wait, Mr. Robeson," my aunt Ceil replied,
pressing his hand with practiced ease.
Then the hat-check girl returned to the club,
humming a Paul Robeson hit on the summer breeze.

I WAS THERE, TOO

"To the wrongs that need resistance. To the right that needs assistance. To the future in the distance. Give yourselves."

~ Carrie Chapman Catt,
President of the National Women's Suffrage Association.

LOVE IN A TIME
OF REVOLUTION

We met at the demonstration,
and fell in love during the riot.
I was hooked the moment she took the stage,
voice filled with clarity and purpose,
no need for a megaphone or bullhorn.

I watched her long hair stream behind her
like a flag caught in an autumn wind,
while the winds of change
blew lustily through the crowd.

As the tear gas drifted over us
and the boisterous marchers panicked
and ran helter-skelter,
I grabbed Laura's hand, and we ran
for a McDonald's beckoning shelter.

Over hamburgers and coffee,
we shared our vision for the future.
As she handed me some flyers,
I took her hand as well,
with gentle pressure on fingers slender and strong.

Those fingers tapped ceaselessly on her computer,
writing bold and brilliant articles
for a radical magazine.
She was a young revolutionary,
and I, an older ordinary progressive,
but a future for The People is meant to be shared,
and sharing could be just for two,
as well as for the masses.

By evening, we were teammates,
and teammates have a way of becoming partners.
But when at last I tried to kiss her,
she pulled away like I was a cop in full riot gear.

Weeping, she sat me down
and with trembling hands, showed me
her personal bible:
"Basics of Revolution for Everyone."

"Don't you see?" My comrade pleaded.
"As men and women take the final steps to Revolution,
we will enter a brand new phase of evolution!
Dating and sex will be outmoded,
as old ways and concepts become eroded!"

I thought about her words,
as I walked the empty streets
to my lonely one-bedroom apartment,
night-time company filled by the activists of history.

Her explanation was meant to inspire me
with bold new insights into women's oppression,
but instead they filled me with an odd depression.

When I reached my building,
I suddenly smiled
in the amber glow of an old streetlamp.
My loneliness vanished
like the cold and damp.
I was entering the next phase of my evolution:
A warrior for non-romantic love, in a time of revolution!

Riding My Pro-Choice Caravan to Freedom

Two brave groups of women and men
climbed aboard two rickety vans
on opposite sides of the country,
and met in the middle.

In each city that welcomed them,
they unfurled the banners
of a new kind of army,
soldiers in a new war
older than they had ever known:

The War On Women,
a battle waged for as long as time,
with the warriors of oppression and patriarchy
about to be defeated without mercy
by the soldiers of sisterhood:

Mothers and daughters,
grandmothers who carried the family's secret shame,
college students who had never grown up
in a country without reproductive choice,
activists from their parent's generation who remembered
the back-alley butchers, the disapproving stares
of emergency room doctors,
the cold jail cells where silence rang in women's ears
and guilt was their only companion.

The Abortion Rights Freedom Ride
called to mind those other freedom rides
throughout the South,
where men and women in buses
faced night-riders with crosses,
and right and wrong was as clear as black and white.

In each city they came to,
the abortion freedom riders unfurled the banners
of their clarion-call: A FETUS IS NOT A BABY!
WOMEN ARE NOT INCUBATORS!
ABORTION IS NOT MURDER!
And their flyers and brochures contained the bullets of truth
fired at the forces of Patriarchy and misogyny.
They traveled South through a modern topography of terror:
In Montana, a clinic firebombed beyond repair.
In Kansas, where a doctor was murdered in his own church
for proclaiming, "Women need abortions, and I'm going to do them!"
Through the darkness to Tennessee and Arkansas,
with their "fetal pain" laws,
and finally to Texas, that brutal headquarters
of the War on Women.

In Texas, they marched, sat in, got arrested,
and brought thousands of women into the streets
to call out and shout down a governor whose words
rang with pious hypocrisy about the sacredness of every life
and the safety of every woman.

They won in Texas,
bringing defeat to a dreadful new law,
and I will be with them every new step of the journey,
taking the fight to the courts and the governor's mansions,
to the clinics who embrace us with a deafening cheer,
to the antis who fear our message loud and clear!

Forced motherhood is female enslavement!
Pro-choice is female empowerment!
Unleash the fury of women as a mighty force for revolution!
Smash Patriarchy and Pornography as a mighty force for evolution!

To the patriarchs and pornographers,
to the gay marriage bashers and clinic trashers,
to the subway flashers and birth-control slashers,
to the women-haters and sex slave traders,
we say: THE FUTURE IS NOT YOURS!
WE WILL WIN THE WAR ON WOMEN!

QUESTIONS BEFORE THE SIT-IN

I watched my friends leave
for the occupation,
and I felt sad.
Students were leaving in droves,
heavy knapsacks strapped tight
to youthful shoulders,
and I was leaving only for my next class.

It was a sit-in at the Seabrook Nuclear Power Plant,
and I chose to stay at school
because I didn't yet have the power
to gently break the law.

So I hugged my best friend goodbye
and sat on a bench,
hugging myself and wanting to cry.
Then like an activist angel,
another friend stopped and asked me why,
inviting me to a protest so nearby!

It was an occupation all our own,
an administration building we called home,
to force our college to invest only in education,
and divest from South Africa's racist segregation.

I had been part of the core group
from my first college days,
and when my friend told me the details
I excitedly agreed.

Then I told her I had one small question
before I packed my bag
for my own march into history:
Why keep it from me for eight long months,
when I had joined the group on day one?
"We had our reasons,"

My friend said with cryptic politeness
and political correctness.
"I didn't agree with them.
Don't try to find out."
She assured me that my loyalty
was never on the table,
yet my group had planned the whole action
under the table!

I was a valued member of the occupation,
but my question stayed a pre-occupation:
I was trusted to share the risks and choices,
and even share our group's advances.
But the activist devil is in the details,
and my leadership qualities were seen as frail.

I Saw What I Should
Have Seen Long Ago

I went to Seattle for the March for Women's Lives,
and the only life I saved was my own.
I went there gleefully, as usual not caring
that I was in no shape to be marching for several miles
when I could barely make it up a steep hill.

I was out of breath, out of shape and out of mind,
and my best friend begged me not to go.
But as always, I made it more important to be helping others
than look at myself and know much help I needed.

So I set out next day with posters and stubbornness,
and my best friend sat beside me in silence on the way,
knowing she could not talk sense into me
and hoping against hope that I could prove her wrong.

But she was so right!

The only marching I did that day
was straight into the pavement
on a steep, rain-slicked Seattle hill,
but I was the only one who slipped.

As I lay unconscious on the pavement,
face bloody and foolish pride gone,
illusions vanished with the pain of impact
and reality began to creep into a mind
that had long ago locked that door.

In Los Angeles, I stopped my games
and went first thing to Urgent Care.
That was the reality check I so urgently needed.
Deep within my injured face,

A tumor was growing.
No one could tell me how long it had been there,
but everyone told me that it was big.

When I got I home,
I went to the bathroom and vomited in fear.
How could I, who cared daily about changing the world,
have missed so many changes that happened to me?

Then I looked in the mirror,
and I saw what I should have seen long ago:
A strange old man stared back at me,
tired and fat and gray,
instead of a vibrant youth at middle age,
still ready to take the world by storm.

The mirror lied to me through the years,
or maybe it just reflected what I begged to see.
I never saw the face in the looking-glass grow lines
deepened by poor choices,
or my once-beautiful hair,
black and strong as a stallion in the fields,
turn slowly pepper-and-salt,
now finally white as a winter moon
above a forest of loneliness and shadows.

As multiple chins cascaded from my ample neck,
and gravity tugged the bags of my stomach
closer to my feet,
I steamed the mirror thoroughly
before stepping from the shower,
and drying myself hurriedly
before an image ghostly and indistinct.

As single ads went unanswered,
dates disappeared,
and invitations from friends dried up
like the summer dust,

I asked the mirror defiantly,
"Mirror, mirror, on the wall,
who's a bachelor for them all?"

"You are, my friend,"
the mirror intoned,
"It is your destiny, your karma,
to find love in a special way,
as your father needs you more each passing day.
Now you, yourself, grow old and out of breath at 58,
and your dreams of youth
arrive too late!"

But at 58, I peered long and hard at the mirror,
and saw what I should have seen long ago:
A mirror only reflects the truth,
it does not predict the future,
or seal our fate.

Perhaps there is still time
to turn things around,
to stand tall and proud before my bones creak
like rusty doors harassed by the wind.

Perhaps there is still time to see a reflection
of someone healthy and strong,
hair gleaming richly,
eyes shining brightly,
wearing the clothes of men,
not hiding beneath bulky sweaters eaten by holes
that would make the homeless cringe.

The mirror has shown me
what I should have seen long ago,
but now I shall look each day
for the man I still can be,
my past a harmless memory,
my future aglow!

Silver Is as Good as Gold

The medal sits upon my mantle,
a silver circle as shiny as the moon.

For years I nurtured fantasies
of winning a medal as golden as the sun,
a constant reminder of what I thought
could only be a dream.

In 2014, I took the first small step
toward making a dream come true.
A friend published my book of poems,
a message to the world in ink of blue.

It was a slender volume speaking truth to power,
human rights poems reflecting my soul
in words raining down like a summer shower.

For three long years I entered contests,
sending my book to everyone
I thought might care about my caring views.

For three long years I labored in silence,
undiscovered but always patient,
unacknowledged but ever-hopeful.

Then in the fall I got an e-mail,
a weekly newsletter called The Water Cooler,
that heated my blood as it announced the winners
of the Living Now Book Awards.
When I saw my name and book beside the silver,
I began living now with a pride
I had long forgotten.

From that day forth I told everyone I knew,
and many I didn't,
about the medal I had won,
a silver just as good as gold,
as shiny as the sun!

PEARL OF THE ATLANTIC

Like a pearl locked tight
within an unyielding clam,
Cuba has been a shimmering jewel
kept hidden from its mighty northern neighbor
for fifty years,
by the arrogance of our embargo
and the racism of our Manifest Destiny.

For a half-century, America's might
has punished this tiny island
for the overthrow of a dictator
popular in the empire of Washington's halls of power.

Generations of Presidents have called Castro a dictator,
but does anyone remember
how Kennedy refused his hand in friendship,
even as he proudly told the citizens of Berlin,
divided by a high wall,
that he would fight tirelessly for their freedom
and that he, too, was a jelly donut?

Instead of a choker of pearls round the slender neck
of the Lady of Guantanamo,
we have put the slender neck of Cuba
in the chokehold of blockade and sanctions.

But now, with the stroke of a pen,
President Obama has begun to undo a mistake
of historic proportions.
Instead of clinging to balsa-wood rafts and canvas sails,
Cubans can apply by the thousands to come on the silver ships
of their own airline.

Instead of visiting on delegations so restrictive
it takes a whole career change to qualify,
now any American with an open mind

can share a beer with an old fisherman at Hemingway's bar,
or round the bases with Cuba's best home-run hitters.
My visit in 1991 was an act of defiance of my country's policies
when I traveled to Cuba on an education tour,
even though I did nothing more subversive
than confer with teachers
and share cookies and apple juice with children who played
while their mothers worked,
and worked diligently around the school
when it was their mothers' turn to study.

Ah, Cuba, my Cuba! My exquisite neighbor to the South!
How I long to stroll again along Havana's Malecon,
where the blood-stirring rhythms of Latin Jazz
float sweetly on the breeze,
and fishermen toss their nets and private cares
on the patient sea.

How I long to see the giants of Cuban medicine
share their secrets with eager American doctors,
and side by side, find a cure for AIDS or cancer
once and for all,
something that doesn't cost an arm and a leg to try.

Times are finally changing,
and a new tide is rolling in.
Soon I can welcome it on the soft dunes of Varadero Beach,
and hum, lustily and off-key, "Guantanamera,"
on the hot cobblestones of Havana, and no one will mind
because they can tell that, yes indeed, I care a lot for the Lady,
Pearl of the Atlantic!

WHEN POLITICIANS LIE,
OUR CHILDREN DIE

Valentine's Day, 2018:
Love was in the air,
but for the students
of Marjory Stoneman Douglas High School,
death rode the wind on that fateful afternoon.

A masked gunman,
formerly one of their own,
laid waste to students, teachers and coaches alike,
even three who gave their own lives
to save the boys and girls they loved.

The seventeen so cruelly cut down
and the seventeen brutally wounded
in body, mind and soul,
have become everyone's son, daughter,
brother, sister, boyfriend, girlfriend.

Even I, safe and far away
in my Los Angeles home,
grieved for these young people
more personally than I expected.

One of the fourteen-year-old girls,
her life stolen before her own adulthood
could even begin,
was the favorite babysitter
of my cousin's grandchildren.

Now these two children she looked after
like an angel
have decorated their rooms with drawings
of their young friend in heaven.

What has been the result of such insanity?
After the shooting stopped, the prayers began.
On national television,
politicians hugged stunned survivors,
attended more funerals of children
than the mind can grasp,
and made pious speeches about gun control.

Still others proclaimed
that the time was not yet right
to talk about gun control,
just about healing and coming together.

How can we come together,
when there isn't even an age limit
on killing each other,
and no ban on buying a rifle to kill a hundred
with one small change?

When politicians lie, our children die.
When brave students traveled hours to Tallahassee
to hear their legislators ban assault rifles,
all they heard was an assault on their intelligence.

The legislature claimed there was no time to debate it,
because it was more urgent to declare pornography
a public health emergency.

After all, guns don't kill people;
sex does.

When the NRA shoots forth
with political might,
our politicians shoot themselves in the foot,
and the Second Amendment comes first
over saving lives.

Parkland, Florida now joins
a new map of terror
in a uniquely American landscape of tragedy.

So many places, so many lives!

When politicians lie, our children die.
I wonder if words few of us knew before Las Vegas,
like "Bump stock" and "AR-15 Assault Rifle,"
will be added to the vocabulary lists
that next year's students
will memorize and be tested on.

At eighteen, we can send our children to die
in foreign wars,
or they can wander into local gun stores
and buy the same rifle they will use
to kill other teenagers in combat.

In many states, they cannot even buy a beer,
but they can buy a rifle to kill a deer –
or each other.

The NRA assures us
that the Second Amendment rules the land.
The AR-15 assault rifle is meant to kill
only people, not deer.

But hunting is legal, and a hunter of people
can kill a classroom of unarmed teenagers
as easily as a herd of deer.

When politicians lie, our children die.
There is no gun control, only mind control!

The hottest new proposal: give weapons to teachers
and other "responsible adults."
Turn our schools into armed fortresses!
But what will happen when a well-trained teacher-soldier
suddenly snaps in class?

The climate is slowly changing,
and in America, there is global warming
towards gun control.
When politicians lie, our children will die no more!

Across the nation, students are studying.
Learning. Listening. Marching. Soon they will vote!
The students of Marjory Stoneman Douglas High School
have had their eyes opened too wide
to have the wool pulled over them again!

Throughout this land,
young people unite and demand:
Action, not just prayers!
Taking stock of the future, not bump stocks!
Real gun control, not mind control!

Speaking with one voice, one heart, one mind!
Marching for their lives –
and they are fearless and tireless.

We must all march with them,
because the future is theirs
and they can change it for us all!

THE GHOSTS OF LATIN AMERICA

"No human being is illegal. That is a contradiction in terms. They can be beautiful or more beautiful, fat or skinny, right or wrong, but Illegal? No human being is illegal!"

~ Elie Wiesel,
writer, human rights activist, Holocaust Survivor

CROSSES TO BEAR

A thousand white crosses
bearing a thousand black-lettered names,
carried by mourners 3,000 strong.

The names are from every country
in Latin America,
but the mourners are from every state
in North America,
walking before a mass grave with a harmless name:
The School of the Americas. Of all the Americas.

This university without walls
is a place where Latin America's military elite
are sent to learn the best our government has to offer:
How to interrogate with torture, but leave the victim alive.
How to kidnap resistance fighters,
and extort the families for huge ransom payments
instead of resistance. starvation, burning villages.
In Vietnam, we called it "Scorched Earth."

It's all there,
it's all true.
The training manuals were updated in '92.

Our intelligence elite teaches modern methods
of counterinsurgency,
while our own universities steadily lose funding,
and charge fees many students cannot pay.

Our government won't reveal the names
of the distinguished faculty of the SOA,
but the black-printed names
on the stark white crosses speak volumes
about the quality of the training:

Hector Davila, El Salvador, aged two.
Shot in the head.
Emilio Rojas, Honduras, age 90

found by family in mass grave.
Violetta Alvarez, Guatemala, aged 15.
Raped by army soldiers before execution.

Hector Davila, the two-year-old:
What crime can a two-year-old commit
to make him deserve a bullet to the head?

The protesters bear their crosses
past a green field and a high hill,
and neat, brick buildings where the students drill.

The mourners try to plant a makeshift cemetery
on the manicured lawns,
but are stopped by the base police.
They try anyway, and are led to waiting buses.
For their crime of gardening,
they are arrested for vandalism.

A mile inside the gates of Fort Benning, Georgia,
where the school occupies a corner of land
most regular soldiers never see,
a dozen buses line the road
to drive us to tents in the dark and cold.

We place the white crosses
with the black letters
in the soft brown earth
by the high green hill.
The crosses are gone,
but the names are there still.

Throughout our lives
we have crosses to bear,
but these names of the dead
with the world we must share.

White crosses carried
with broken hearts,
till the last empty class
of the SOA starts!

December 2nd, 7:30p.m.

7:30 p.m. on a warm December night:
Two women waited with joy and roses
in the airport in San Salvador,
where every passport received a stamp of fear.
As the happily bouncing forms of their Maryknoll sisters
appeared in the crowd,
none of the four women knew
that other eyes were watching them,
stealthily, warily, waiting only to interrupt their journey
before they could cry for help out loud.

In El Salvador, 1980, it was still safe to talk to God,
provided only God could hear.
Any louder, and the Guardia Nacionale might hear,
and silence those who speak and those who listen alike.

By 1980, the priests were dying side by side
with the peasants, sharing communion wine
and clandestine graves.
but they hadn't killed the nuns yet,
and they wouldn't dare kill blonde, blue-eyed North Americans,
or so Jean Donovan believed.
How could they know that within the hour,
they would suffer the same fate as the poor,
to die by the road beneath a moon brighter than winter snow?

Six men of the Guardia, dressed like the very civilians
they terrorized every day,
fell in step behind the nuns
and watched them leave the noise and light.

7:30 p.m.: the road to San Salvador
was long and dark,
a modern road to Calvary for believers in the poor
with their own crosses to bear,
and even Jean's sturdy microbus
could not push back the shadows.

The bright lights of the roadblock
threw the microbus in sharp relief,
headlamps bathing the faces of the soldiers
in halos of their own.

An even darker fork in the road
led to a shallow grave in the newly turned earth,
dug in advance by men who daily bathed their hands
in blood and dirt as though one and the other were the same.

The women cried out,
the earth moaned,
shots rang,
silence quickly returned to rule the night.

For two days, the women were listed only as "missing."
The news suggested they had fled to the mountains,
and the American Secretary of State even opined
that they tried to run a Guardia roadblock
and got caught in a firefight.
Nuns with guns—a theory to make even Jesus
turn over in his own shallow grave.

December 4th: the grave was opened,
the women unearthed and resurrected
for all the world to see and remember,
palm fronds from the mission to shield their faces from the dirt,
a bouquet of Jean's beloved roses in December
to shield their souls from the pain of being forgotten.

NOT EVEN THE COOK WAS SPARED

Six Jesuit men of the cloth prepared
for their weekly day with God,
and 26 men in hiding
prepared to send them home
to God forever.

The resident priests at the University of Central America
worked late into the afternoon,
each busy at a special task:
There was Padre Ignacio Ellacuria,
writing a sermon of liberation theology
no words would ever hear,
but he felt liberated nonetheless.

Padre Ignacio Martin-Baro,
psychologist as well as priest,
researched a paper on the psychology of torture victims,
and how to help them heal –
information subversive to a government
that depended on torture to survive.

Padre Segundo Montes,
expert in migration studies,
rested after his repatriation
of a whole new village of refugees,
returning in defiance to bury their dead
and bring to life fields of corn and sweet potatoes,
where soldiers once planted bodies and plowed them
in neat rows of newly turned earth.

The other brothers tended to the garden
or prepared the table for the simple meal
that marked the end of the day
in service to the poor.

Padre Joaquin Lopez y Lopez
lit the votive candles in the humble chapel.

Padre Armando Lopez visited the library,
his sharp mind teased by a question
posed by St. Paul many centuries before.

Padre Juan Ramon Moreno gave a blessing
and a greeting to Elba Ramos,
their excellent cook, and her daughter Celina,
a sixteen-year-old beauty
whose prospects for love and marriage were marred
by the lack of young men
the government had not yet stolen
for the civil war.

To the men of the Atlacatl Battalion,
hiding in a nearby building with a clear view of the church,
the men of the cloth were "red priests,"
subversives who had turned their backs
on the true teachings of Christ
and sold their souls to the blasphemy of Marx.

And that Padre Ellacuria,
now he was the worst!
He kept criticizing the government,
kept calling for negotiations with the guerrillas,
kept polluting the minds of the poor with lies
that they could inherit the Beloved Community
right here on Earth!

He was dangerous, alright,
all the Fathers were,
for raising the hopes of the pueblo,
when hope was surely the work of the Communist Devil!
They had to be taught a lesson.
They had to be silenced.

So the men of the Battalion moved in speed and silence,
this rapid response force created by the United States,
and searched the buildings of the university one by one.
When they got to the residence of the priests,
they tried to force their way in,
but the priests deprived them of their sport.
Perhaps, being priests,
they sensed that their homecoming
with the One True Peacemaker
was near at hand,
and they willingly opened their doors to the soldiers.

One priest,
one bullet from an AK-47,
one at a time,
and each priest fell silently where he stood
on sacred ground.

Then the army searched the rooms,
and the dormitories,
and the chapel,
even the kitchen,
and at last they were rewarded with the shaking forms
of Elba and Celina,
who had taken what refuge they could
beneath the farthest reaches of the long dining table.

The Commander made them lie flat,
and fired at their heads point blank,
as a well-trained officer should.

Then, because they were witnesses
too dangerous to leave to fate,
he fired two more shots to finish them off:
Elba, whose simple meals the priests called "heaven-sent,"
and Celina, just sixteen – the same age as Anne Frank,
wrapped in the soft linen of the table cloth,
now a blood-stained funeral shroud.

The soldiers vanished in the night, their task complete,
and all was still again.
The grass, heavy with blood, bent in the dark wind,
the doors and walls were pockmarked with bullet-holes
like bizarre pieces of modern art,
and on one wall, a cardboard sign hung
to record a coward's lie:
"FMLN EXECUTED THOSE WHO INFORMED ON IT.
THEIR DEATH, THE PEOPLE'S VICTORY."

The shuttered doors swung lazily to and fro,
and eight more bodies were added to a list already so high
the nation stared,
on a mission carried out in such soldierly fashion,
not even the cook was spared.

FOR GRANDMOTHER,
WHO TAUGHT ME WHO I AM

Gracias siempre, mi abuela,
for helping me learn who I am.
I am grown up now
and you have grown old,
and the years have not been kind
to either of us,
but still I know who I am.

Your feet are tired and sore
from your endless marches
'round the Plaza de Mayo,
and my 27-year-old heart
feels old and sore from fighting the loss
of all that I thought I once was.

I still remember the dark afternoon
when you came to me in the mist
of a Buenos Aires thunderstorm,
and soothed my childish tears
when I skinned my knee on the wet pavement.

You kissed the hurt and made me smile again,
as mothers and grandmothers know how to make pain mend.
Then you stared long and hard at a photo
that showed the face of a mystery without end.

You put it carefully in your purse that first time,
and turned away from my questioning eyes.
But as the months passed and my questions continued,
at last you showed me the picture of a laughing young woman,
and my face went pale and my laughter ceased, as I saw myself!

"Who is she?" I whispered,
trying to keep my voice from breaking.
You looked at me with the saddest eyes I had ever seen,
and said, "She's my daughter, Liliana.
The government said she was ripe for the taking!"

"She is lost," you explained,
and at first I did not understand.
Then before bed, I sang a nursery rhyme that said,
"In the land-of-I-don't-remember,
I take three steps and I'm lost,"
and I wanted to bury my head deep in sand.

Would I be lost like Liliana,
if I took a step this way, and wondered if I may?
If I took one step over there,
and got a big scare?
What if I took a backward step fast?
Would it be my last?

You came one night to my home,
and I listened to you talk
through my partly closed door.
"She is my grand-daughter! I have her papers,"
you demanded,
and showed the same picture, so my parents would be sure.

"We had nothing to do with the Disappeared Ones,"
my father shouted in reply.
He stamped his feet in rage, and swore.
He shook his fist at you, and said,
"Now leave this house, and come no more!"

I was only seven, and cried in bed,
my mind aflame,
my body shaking.
Would I become like Liliana,
just another girl the government said
was ripe for the taking?
I shed many tears and hated you then,
but I watched you march for endless years.
You stayed apart from me, but always smiled,
until one day, I cast aside my youthful fears.

The junta was gone,
but you and I were left, *abuela*.
Like a shadow army,
the *Desaparecidos* were returning to life,
and my mother's ghost marched with you,
through fragile peace and lingering strife.

The history books we children learned from
were written by assassins,
and only the physical remnants
could call forth the truth.

So we walked arm in arm
through the old concentration camp
in the Navy School of Mechanics,
where the only classes taught were the mechanics of death.

You showed me the birthing cell in the basement,
and released a scream you could no longer suppress.
This was the iron bed on which Liliana gave birth,
and clutched my tiny arms as I was torn from her breast.

At night, we stood by the banks of the Rio de la Plata,
beneath a full moon and the distant thump
of a helicopter's blades.
I wondered if a helicopter just like it had dumped my mother
in these river swells of burnished silver,
or the wine-purple crests of the Atlantic's waves.

I was given to two good people:
My mother an architect and my father, a four-star general.
I believe them when they still plead innocent
of any crimes against the disappeared.
But I am no longer afraid that I, too, will disappear.
I am not afraid to take one step this way,
and wonder if I may.
To take a step over there
is no more a big scare.

Even if my country is still the land-of-I-don't-remember,
I can take three steps and never be lost,
because I will always remember.
I am a daughter of Argentina,
Isabel Beltran.
Thank you, *abuela*,
for teaching me who I am!

WHY DO YOU CALL ME "ILLEGAL"?

When you call me an "illegal alien,"
I feel like an outlaw from another planet.
Only, I didn't come in a flying saucer,
I walked all night across the desert with my parents.
How can any human being be illegal?
Why do you call me that, when you don't even know me?

The sticks of your police batons
and the stones thrown through my parents' windows
can break my bones,
but your words can hurt me most of all!

Is it my fault that my parents crossed the border
when I was only four?
I was not consulted on that decision.
We did not come to steal your jobs,
or even seek asylum from the civil war
that tore my country apart.

We came seeking only the asylum of a better life,
a chance to raise ourselves up
in a home with two bedrooms,
with a roof that doesn't collapse in the winter rains,
and floors we don't have to share
with three chickens and two goats.

I remember as if it was yesterday
the endless journey from our country to yours.
In Mexico, I remember the cold dust of the Sonoran Desert,
and the great, tall shadows of the saguaro cactus,
with arms outstretched like monsters
seeking to devour us.

Mama made a papoose like the Indians do,
with straps around her waist so she could carry me
when my small feet gave way on the ten-mile trek,
and I rested my weary head on her back.

I have done well in America
since that long night of walking.
I am an *indocumentada,*
an undocumented young woman,
who earned straight-A's
and became Student Body President in high school.

In my second year of college,
I am now the lead female dancer in the ballet corps,
and I have won a gold medal in freestyle swimming.
I am smart, beautiful and loving.
Would you really turn down a date with me,
because your government calls me "illegal"?

Last week, *La Migra* came for us.
In my mind, I hear the engines of the deportation plane,
and I am so afraid.
Something your President calls the Dream Act
may let me stay another year or two
so at least I can finish college,
but my poor parents may be sent home tomorrow!

Yes, I am a dreamer,
but I would never dream of harming you.
I dream only of a happy life for myself,
and a much better one for my parents,
who have sacrificed so much for me.

This country has been our home for twenty years.
We have no other home!
When *La Migra* came for my parents,
and handcuffed them before my eyes,
I cried all night,
and searched all the next day
for a lawyer to help me.

The last thing my parents said to me,
as I blew them kisses through their cell bars
in the detention center, was:
"Stay strong. In El Salvador or America,
your spirit is not wrong!"

Call me a refugee, and I might agree with you.
Call me "undocumented," and I can live with that.
But never again look me in the eyes,
and call me "illegal."

It is your words and your laws that rob me of my humanity,
and reduce me to that outlaw from another planet,
when you call an "illegal alien."
But guess what? I am legally on this planet to stay,
and no human being, anywhere, is "illegal"!

To an Unknown Artist, Sent to the Tower

The oakwood tower stands firm and strong
above the grounds of the old concentration camp,
now a peace garden,
once a place meant to silence
Chile's most vocal critics.

Within the tower walls, ten microcells,
each 3 X 7 feet,
housed the most dangerous prisoners:
The artists, who painted hidden canvasses
of mourners honoring the slaughtered of a military coup,
close-up portraits of faces etched in pain and fear,
wondering if they will be the next to disappear.

Dangerous, too, are the Victor Jaras of every country,
writing songs to inspire the masses
to take to the streets,
and break down walls with their voices.

Then there are the poets,
writing verses that speak to people
in the language of liberation,
of struggle as a name for hope.

Strange to think that before Pinochet's coup,
The Villa Grimaldi was a gathering place
for artists of every stripe.

They congregated weekly to share their vision
in a true Teatro Campesino,
a theater open to the whole community,
and a university without walls open to everyone
truly seeking higher learning.

Yet as soon as fascism spreads its dark fingers
in any country,
silencing every challenge raised by free expression,
canvas by canvas,
symphony by symphony,
poems by each revolutionary verse,
it is always the artists who are first to face the stranglehold.

When the Nazis extinguished the bright light
of liberating thought,
they built a concentration camp called Terezin
especially for the artists and intellectuals.

By day they wore the blue and white striped uniforms,
but by night, those fingers not yet broken
painted portraits of a sad old greybeard with working gums
or a child desperate to catch a last butterfly.

And what of you, unknown artist sent to the tower
of a nameless camp or prison today?
As you sit hunched in your windowless cell,
what subversive art did you bring forth
to land you in such hell?

Perhaps in vivid color you brought to life a great canvas,
showing the masses in struggle and victory.
Perhaps you remembered Violetta Para's "Gracias a La Vida,"
humming the melody of "Thanks for Life"
to your fellow prisoners, even as life itself was daily robbed
of all reason to be thankful.

Or perhaps you shared a crowded bench with Victor Jara
in the soccer stadium of Santiago,
helping his shattered hands compose "Estadio Chile,"
seeking to score his final points with the people he loved
before the soldiers evened the score
against his game of freedom?

The old concentration camp in Chile is gone now,
and the water tower stands guard over the ghosts within.
The DINA no longer bring their loads of prisoners
for torture and confession to imaginary crimes
against the State.

But in another country and another time,
perhaps even our own,
when freedom of thought is suppressed
and life is no longer free to be displayed
in art that inspires action,
in a new Villa Grimaldi, rage will kindle
at a painter's canvas,
or a musician's throaty clarion call,
or a poet's revolutionary words
that even the tower cannot silence.

IN THE STADIUM WITH VICTOR

There were six of us together
on a hard wooden bench.
But I was nearest to you, Victor,
and I saw it all – saw your end
and our new beginning.

Five thousand of us were jammed
in this small space called the Chile Stadium.
You and I sat above Center Court, Victor,
looking down on painted lines
where soccer players danced between each other's legs
and bounced goals from heads hard enough
to absorb the blows.

But it is one thing to score a goal
with a head of hair,
another to feel the butt of a rifle
crack against the tender skull.

I looked at you,
and saw your gentle face working
in the silent creation of a *Nueva Canción*,
a new song to lift our hopes
after the despair of a coup that took only a day.

There we all were,
exposed to hunger, thirst, pain, insanity.
One of our companions killed himself
by jumping many tiers to the painted floor.
The guards were angered by the mess,
and beat our friend, Alberto, beside us at random,
until he no longer resembled a human being.

But Pinochet's butchers
could not destroy your humanity.
You raised your voice in song, as only Victor Jara can,

and five thousand of us who still had our own voices
began to take up the melody,
and then the potent words.

In your mortal anguish,
you cried out to God:
"What happened to the paradise you created
in just seven days?
These four walls are no Garden of Eden!
This stadium is but a garden for the Serpent
to roam unchecked, and fill our veins with poison."

The Bible tells us how Eve seduced Adam
with a red, shiny apple.
I have not had an apple in months!
All of us in this haunted stadium
can only smell the flowers of evil
and taste the bitter fruit of defeat.

Some guards recognized you
from your people's concerts.
They stormed the bleachers,
and dragged you down the concrete steps
by your curly hair.

Out of spite for your music
that all the working class take up as their call,
the guards pulled out your nails,
smashed your fingers and hands,
then laughing, handed you a guitar, and said,
"Play, bastard, play!"

But a Voice of the Voiceless can never be silenced.
"Victor has left us a new song!" I shouted
to the tattered men and women in every direction.

I held the guitar for you
in your crippled hands.
So we took up the song,

And line by line, stanza by stanza,
we learned it by heart and took it to heart.

With a strength
that only the music of struggle can bring,
you plucked the strings that yielded to you,
and called forth the tune.

And your magnificent poem,
which a whole people have heard or read by now,
was saved by the same five thousand
you wrote it for.

Yes, I was in the stadium with you, Victor.
At all times I was with you,
and I saw your poem "Estadio Chile"
with my own eyes.

We copied it word for word
on scraps of paper
and hid it in our shoes.
With my own stubby feet,
I curled it between my toes.

When your body was found several days later,
there were 40 bullet holes throughout.
The guards left you at the entrance to the stadium,
so all the prisoners would see and be terrified.
But it did not frighten us.
You had already opened our eyes.

Songs of the suffering masses
are not written with pencils
on scraps of paper,
they are composed deep in the soul.

I was in the stadium beside you, Victor,
and your soul still lives.
So do your words,
and the people of Chile will sing them daily,
until the stadium is no longer a concentration camp,
but only a place for sporting events
where everyone is a winner!
As you sang to us untiringly,
Venceremos – we SHALL win!

VICTOR JARA was one of the most beloved folk musicians in Latin America. From the heart of the slum barrios of Chile, he took up the form of NUEVA CANCION, combining traditional peasant and Indian melodies with powerful images of poverty, oppression, and resistance. On September 11, 1973, with military equipment and backing of the United States, Augusto Pinochet overthrew the popular Socialist Democracy of Salvador Allende. Victor was one of the first to be arrested, at the Technical College where he taught, and on September 12th was one of 5,000 people imprisoned in the Chile Stadium – not be confused with the National Stadium, one of the largest detention sites in the country. Victor was tortured and murder in the manner described in this poem, but his spirit lives on among the indigenos and the working class throughout the Americas. Along with legendary singer-songwriter Violetta Para, Victor Jara never lost his voice or his vision for the people. A bullet can silence a person, but never his or her voice. *Venceremos!*

© Reuters/F. Bimmer

WE ARE NOT YOUR HUNTERS

"I have learned from an early age to abjured the use of meat, and the time will come when men such as I will look upon the murder of animals as they now look upon the murder of men"

~ Leonardo da Vinci

BELOVED SATAO,
FELLED BY AN ARROW

You were Lord of the Elephants,
a mighty bull that made the savanna shake
beneath the power of your feet.

When you stretched your trunk high
to knock loose the tender leaves,
the Baobaob tree bowed low to greet you.

When you announced the dawn
with your trumpet call,
the lion and the gazelle
made momentary peace to share the song.

At nearly fifty years of age,
perhaps you remembered a different Africa,
when the tall grass bent in the wind
and the land was green,
and your favorite food was bountiful
as far as your eyes could see.

But the ground has turned hot and dry,
the grass has turned gold and fallow
and crunches underfoot,
the life-giving thunderclouds retreat,
and Man encroaches.

This year, the rains came late,
and you wandered far in search of food.
As you slaked your thirst
and cooled your skin and tired feet at last,
you were too enthralled to see the danger
hidden in the tall reeds so close behind.

The poachers donned combat fatigues
and crept with practiced stealth
through the underbrush at the water's edge.
Taking careful aim,
they let loose with weapons that made no sound,
except the screams you could not suppress
as the heavy arrows found their mark.

The poisoned dart struck deep
above your mighty flanks,
and your bellow of anguish shook the savanna
from end to end.

But the poachers heard nothing
but their own cry of victory,
as they rushed forth to claim the ivory treasure
by which you were justly known.

Your great tusks resisted the saw and the knife,
and it took those who loved you ten long days
to identify your corpse and stand guard
beside your mutilated face,
with tears streaming down their own.

Beloved Satao,
Lord of the Elephants,
no more will your tusks,
so long they touched the ground,
scrape the tender bark from tall trees,
and lift the grass in great tufts to your laughing jaws.

Those ivory tributes to your reign
that awed tourists on safari
and scientists on survey alike,
are but a memory now,
a trinket on someone's distant mantelpiece
or a King and Queen fit for an ornate chessboard.
But in your five-and-forty years,
you made elephant-love
to dozens of eager mates.
Perhaps your genes live on
in the many babies that flap their outsized ears
to cool themselves,
and dutifully follow their mothers across the endless plains.

Beloved Satao, felled by a poisoned arrow,
your spirit still rules in Mother Africa,
and your offspring, now fierce and strong,
will surely help all that you once were
to trod the soft cool grass again, in worlds without end.

THE LION AND THE DENTIST

When you strode lazily across the savannah
for your morning exercise,
the tall grass bent beneath the power of your paws.
When you let loose your mighty roar,
all living things took heed, for none could doubt
that you were the Lion King.

To awed humans
who came to love and respect you,
you were not Simba,
but Cecil.

With your great black mane
and deceptively sleepy eyes,
you drew onlookers from around the world
who took a hundred photos of you
in a hundred poses,
but none could truly capture
your regal beauty.

But thousands of miles
from the grasslands of Zimbabwe,
in a land you never knew of,
a man polished not his camera
but a rifle, with high-powered bullets
and a bow and arrows to bow your royal head.

He was a dentist
whose job was pulling teeth,
but whose lifelong passion
was pulling teeth as keepsakes
from creatures far larger than he.

He had hunted most things
that can hunt you,
and surely his home was decorated

with rich pelts and mounted heads
with forlorn eyes,
but he had always longed to take down a lion.

You were the undisputed King of the Jungle,
so he, a hunter of but modest size
who would be easy prey for a lion to kill,
packed his rifle and his favorite safari clothes
and flew to the other side of the world
to make his sporting dream come true.

His trip and guide cost him $50,000,
so he prayed for success and paid for the best.
He and his guide lured you,
ah, lured you,
perhaps with the bait of a fresh kill,
outside the National Park that protected you.

No ordinary hunter,
the dentist drew back the taut strings of a heavy bow,
and let an arrow fly.
It struck deep into your flank,
and your famous roar became a bellow of pain.

For a day and a half
the dentist followed your bloody tracks,
searching without respite
for the telltale signs of a wounded lion.

When they found you beneath a baobaob tree,
you were too weak to run or even stand,
and the dentist ended your pain
with a single bullet he could boast of
till the end of his days.
What makes a man
fill a gun with lead,
and fire it at
a living creature's head?

The dentist paused for a victory photo
with his expensive guide,
his hunter's face suffused with pride,
while your loyal pride searched the savannah
and your cubs played freely,
unaware that you had died.

The dentist claims he now regrets it,
not knowing he was killing you.
But that makes little difference,
for Zimbabwe has lost its favorite son
and the dentist has the lion's head he won.

GOING TO THE DOGS

The cages were placed in a circle
on the sawdust-covered floor.
Around them stood men, some grim,
others laughing boisterously with a whiskey in hand.

There was much drinking and laying of wagers
in the cellar of a nameless bar,
on a street the spectators had already forgotten.
All they remembered was the money to be made,
and the fame to be won for the owner,
when man's best friend
became man's best fighter.

The cages were opened
for the main fight of the evening.
The two dogs eyed each other warily,
sniffing and circling,

Then growling with throaty menace.
The owners and the spectators shouted
at the tops of their voices,
and all at once,
and the harried bet-taker tried to make sense
and keep track, as names and dollars and odds
filled the air and a legal pad from end to end.

The dogs reared on hind legs,
and bit deep into each other's flesh.
Screams of canine anguish were muffled
as the jaws of one fighter clamped firmly
on the snout of the other.

The spectators shouted and cheered,
money and liquor flowed hard and fast,
and the fighting dogs lost themselves
in the primal heat of combat.
They had moved beyond pain now;
each wanted only to kill and win.

The owner of the spotted pit bull
smiled inwardly with relief.
His dog was smaller but quicker
than the Red-Eyed Demon,
and the tide of battle was turning.

With a last blow from a heaving chest,
the Memphis Mangler landed atop the bigger and older dog,
and its owner, who seemed unprepared
for violence on this level,
quickly conceded.

The opposing dogs, made hungry for two days
and kept in the tightest of cages to make them vicious,
were now wrapped tenderly in soft blankets
and whisked to the care of well-paid vets,
who for a piece of the action
would render them safe to fight again.

The spectators drifted away,
commenting on the fight.
Already plans for a rematch were agreed
on the most generous of terms,
and the word would be out by morning
on the underground circuit.

The victorious owner of the Memphis Mangler
looked at his oozing flanks,
and stroked the dog's wounded side.
"It'll be alright, boy," he whispered reassuringly.
"Food and water is waiting for you,
and plenty of pills to ease your pain."
The dog whimpered gratefully,
and thumped his tail weakly
on the floor of a now-much bigger cage.

The battle was over,
and once again man's best fighter
and man's best champion
was man's bloody but faithful best friend.

MIRACLE IN THE HARBOR

The glassy swells heaved ashore
with the echo of thunder,
a symphony of the sea applauded at every note
by hundreds of onlookers on the pier.

My parents and I were among the crowd.
We had come that morning to Seal Beach,
La Jolla's landmark that belonged without dispute
to the fat harbor seals that drew viewers like a magnet
from across the beaches of California.

The seals catch the sun's warm rays
and bark at visitors,
who strain from every vantage point
for a photo to remember.

But today the waves
were the stars of the show,
and even the seals
did not challenge their domain.

They hugged the shore,
cooling their skins from the blazing sun,
but refraining from their lazy,
ever graceful, fun.

Suddenly, between the hills of white and green,
a small gray form appeared.
A baby seal had tried to prove its worth
and dared the limits of the foam,
but lost his way
and couldn't make the long swim home.

His mother woke
and dove from shore,
her frantic bark
a fearsome roar.

Rescue plans swept through our crowd.
A dozen ideas were shared aloud.
One man jumped in, but nearly drowned.
We hauled him out without a sound.

Someone threw a juicy fish
that landed an inch
from the baby's nose,
but the seal pup's eyes began to close.

Then with a groan and a mighty thump
that made the whole pier and our hearts jump,
a rescue boat sliced through the waves,
a harbor seal pup's life to save.

The patrol boat turned into the crests,
hoping good luck would do the rest.
The baby found the strength to swim,
even though the odds were slim.

The rescuers played a tape of an adult seal,
and lifted the baby on the boat
when its strength gave out
and it began to float.

They dried it gently with a towel,
and held it till they reached the beach.
The mother stared suspiciously,
then knew her baby was in reach.

The rescuers laid the baby
in the sand,
and fed both seals
some fish by hand.

The mother pushed her pup
further from the deadly sea,
then kissed its face
for all to see!

TIME FOR GOODBYE

"I'm not afraid of being dead. I'm just afraid of what you might have to go through to get there."

~ Pamela Bone

A Gentle Way Out

So my beloved daughter,
the time has come
for you to say goodbye,
though you still have so much to live for!

We lived near the beach,
and as a child you already loved the sea,
and everything in it.
I watched you darting fearlessly
between the waves,
as graceful as the dolphins
who played by the shore.

You were happy as a child,
happy all through the challenges
of school and college.
There was a brightness in you
that warmed us like the sun,
and hid the shadow deep within you.

When the pains began,
none of us thought they were serious.
You had a fine boyfriend
who had the inside track
on becoming a fiancé,
and you even joked that maybe you were pregnant.

A growth was taking root deep inside,
but it wasn't a baby.
In the dark mystery of your private feminine parts,
a tumor was forming.

When our family doctor,
who loved you like a daughter,
called us to his office,
his face was ashen as he gave us the news.

The Ovarian cancer was far along,
And winning this fight would be long and hard.
The radiation and chemotherapy ravaged your body,
But never your spirit,
And your soul stayed as bright as the sun.

But one dark day,
when the pills made you very sick,
you took my hand
and told me in the gentlest voice
that you wanted a gentle way out.

"I don't want to leave you
when the tumor tells me I'm ready,
or the doctors say it's time to prepare,"
you told me with firmness and control.

I cried for many nights,
and prayed that you would change your mind.
But slowly I knew you were right –
everyone deserves a gentle way out.

Our state did not allow a doctor
to help a patient leave this world,
only to help a child come into it
or an adult to stay in it, willingly or not.

So I began to research a subject
I never thought I'd live to know about.
I traveled south of the border, to Mexico,
where I found the clinics I'd read of.

The ones that prescribed strong drugs to humans
had nothing to prescribe for me but quiet directions
to the veterinary clinics,
where the animal doctors could prescribe relief
for the largest pets,
to help them sleep forever.

The animal medicines would work for you,
but supposedly they tasted terrible!
I could not bear to think that the last look
on your sweet face
would be a grimace.

Next I flew to Switzerland,
where I learned of a group
that secretly helped people
who were seeking a gentle way out.

I mingled in the European beauty
of Zurich and Geneva,
walked and meditated beneath the glaciers
of the Matterhorn, high above Zermatt.

But when I showed you the pictures,
you gave me a long, sad smile.
"I don't want to die in a land where I am a stranger,
however welcome.
I don't want to die beneath the high, cool mountains,
however beautiful,
whose peaks are as far out of reach
as the treatments that may save me."

You told me that you were a child of the sea,
a playmate of the dolphins,
a musician of the waves,
playing a symphony whose rhythms were the drumbeats
of the dancing swells.

So we moved to Oregon,
where a gentle way out was legal,
set as law by the courage of the voters
who stood up to doctors and senators alike.

I bought a lovely house on the Oregon coast,
overlooking the sea you loved so much.
For two blessed months, we filled the rooms
with all your memories,
and made new ones to fill the long years
of the future.

We hired a caretaker to push your wheelchair
to the beach below,
where you would still able to walk upon the sand.
We took long drives to enchanted forests below Mt. Hood,
and rode a hot-air balloon in the golden glow
of early skies.

We never stopped the treatments and hoped for a miracle,
but miracles are harder to come by
than sudden disaster.

One day you told me,
with sadness in your sapphire eyes
and surprising strength still in your hand,
that your time had come.

I did not argue with you,
only called the doctor who bravely agreed to help,
one of the two who had to painfully declare
that hope was lost.

We gathered in the living room,
and drew back the curtains
to reveal the beach and the sea
that were your home away from home.
Your mom and I, and Joseph,
who would have been your fiancé,
kissed you softly on the cheek
and stood side by side,
arms locked around each other's waists.

The doctor gave your pills
to help you sleep,
then a merciful needle
to help you keep sleeping.
Our hearts were broken but spirits strong,
for we knew your decision was not wrong.

From a woman's pain
we are given life,
but why must death
be with pain and strife?

Politics and medicine have no right
to tell us how, and when, to say farewell.
If all who live have a right to cry,
then surely we have the right to die.
We start our lives with a slap and a shout,
but we all have the right
to a gentle way out.

BIOGRAPHY

Henry Howard I have been a Los Angeles peace and justice poet since the earliest days of the online literary anti-war protest, Poets Against the War, started by publisher and poet Sam Hamill, in February, 2003. Much of my writing, from poetry to articles and a historical novel-in-progress, is linked by themes of human rights and social justice – just like my life! I will always remember Martin Sheen's famous clarion call to action at the first School of the Americas protest I attended in Ft. Benning, GA in 1998: "You all know what I do to earn a living, but this is how I live!" Like Martin, this is how I live, because I know no other way until the world truly changes for the better.

I am proud to have my work represented by VAGABOND. Like the vagabond himself, with tall pointed hat, knapsack full of books, and sturdy walking stick, we are all wanderers in search of doing a greater good through revolutionary poetry, and peace activism. In 2016, my first collection, *Sing to Me of My Rights*, also published by VAGABOND, was honored with the silver medal in the Living Now Book Awards, Evergreen Medal for World Peace. It is my greatest hope that this slender volume moves people at the same level as my first book – because this is how we live.

DEDICATIONS

This book is dedicated, as always, to my amazing parents, Alice and Alfred Howard, both of whom have passed on, but neither of whom went gently into that good night. They both cared passionately about the human condition, and took pride in bringing me up the same way.

My mother was the closet activist in the family, hardly telling me about it because she felt sick about seeing so little of her peace work come to fruition. When I was in high school, she and a secret group of mothers went weekly to the United Nations, and protested apartheid, racism, and nuclear weapons. My mom was actually a member of Dr. King's Poor People's Campaign and Women's Strike for Peace, and when she was just fourteen, handed out union flyers in Washington Square Park with a close girlfriend. Sometimes they had to flee when companies sent anti-union goon squads to break up the rallies!

Both my parents were members of Leonard Bernstein's "Friends of the Panthers," and I got to meet many famous activists through social events my mother and father took me to. My dad didn't have the luxury of marches and rallies; he had to earn a living, but he admired everything I stood for, even though I gave him a few gray hairs over the years!

This book is also dedicated to my many equally amazing friends who have stood by me throughout the years, and helped form many of my strongest opinions. To name them all would take a book unto itself, and I consider each one essential – so I hope they know who they are.

And lastly, to my wonderful family members, friends as well as relatives, who inspire me and keep me going every day. This book is for all of you! Without you, and my loving friends, I would not be here today – and you know what I mean.

VAGABOND